*f*P

THE
BOY KINGS

A JOURNEY INTO THE HEART

OF THE SOCIAL NETWORK

KATHERINE LOSSE

Free Press
New York   London   Toronto   Sydney   New Delhi

A Note to Readers
Names and identifying details of some of the people portrayed in this book have
been changed.

Free Press
A Division of Simon & Schuster, Inc.
1230 Avenue of the Americas
New York, NY 10020

First Free Press hardcover edition June 2012

FREE PRESS and colophon are trademarks of Simon & Schuster, Inc.

For information about special discounts for bulk purchases, please contact Simon
& Schuster Special Sales at 1-866-506-1949 or business@simonandschuster.com.

The Simon & Schuster Speakers Bureau can bring authors to your live event. For
more information or to book an event, contact the Simon & Schuster Speakers
Bureau at 1-866-248-3049 or visit our website at www.simonspeakers.com.

Designed by Carla Jayne Jones

Manufactured in the United States of America

10   9   8   7   6   5   4   3   2   1

ISBN 978-1-4516-6826-1
ISBN 978-1-4516-6827-8 (ebook)

To

"Shall I project a world?"
—*Thomas Pynchon*

CONTENTS

INTRODUCTION

At the sputtering beginning of this new century we were all, perpetually, waiting for something to happen. After the sudden, unexpectedly fiery morning of 9/11, we developed a new, nonspecific vigilance: a demand to know that some critical event, somewhere, was occurring, however distant. Most things that the cable news reported on after 9/11 seemed irrelevant: a toothless bomb scare here, a prop-plane crash there. We clung to televised surveillance because it was the one thing we could count on: distant wars and threats. To assist our indiscriminate monitoring, cable news created a news ticker that ran underneath the newscast to assure us hourly that yes, somewhere, something terrible had occurred. And, perhaps, because war, unlike understanding and diplomacy, seemed clear and defined, our president started a war, but that didn't work; so he started another war, and that didn't work either. Suddenly, nothing was really working.

I spent the early 2000s nursing a nervous anxiety that reflected the nation's, fed by a general sense of foreboding and by outsized ambition and aimless anticipation—the impulse to do something or be someone at all cost that characterizes one's early twenties. Having graduated from Wesleyan with a degree in English, I found myself in a graduate program at Johns Hopkins that was, I soon discovered, as spectacularly failure-ridden as the new century. My Ph.D. program began golden and full of promise, with the assurance that we would enter easily into the ranks of the elite and tenured professors produced by the top-rated English department. However, constant and sundry department shakeups and scandals left us uneasy and uncertain, and my bright future seemed doomed. Jobs in English departments were dwindling and most Ph.D. students were finding themselves in decade-long holding patterns, waiting for jobs that would never come.

To add to my sense of anxiety, Johns Hopkins was perched atop a hill in Baltimore, which is a bizarre and barren city, especially for someone from Arizona, unfamiliar with the advanced state of America's postindustrial urban decay. Hopkins, we were told proudly in orientation, was the largest employer in the city. The unacknowledged second was the drug trade, supported by the steady stream of heroin flowing through the port. The streets just beyond the campus were full of mayhem, opaque and unreal to the outsider, with men on street corners wearing long white T-shirts whose daily work I would only come to grasp after *The Wire* began airing. As the show's Omar explained, capturing Baltimore city's prescient, postapocalyptic logic perfectly: "It's all in the game." He was right: If we went to Hopkins hoping to indulge in the endless play of academic discourse, what we got instead was a cold education in the hard facts of twenty-first-century American life: wealthy institutions pitted against students, individuals against one another, rampant poverty and violence. No one—not the Hopkins students who were occasionally murdered, nor the grad students whose promised jobs didn't actually exist—was safe anymore.

In response, students I knew at Hopkins developed a streetwise approach to life. "You have to fight crazy with crazy," we told each other before we ventured out on the empty, dangerous streets at night. It was this mode of watchfulness, alert to the sinister and absurd, rather than the lessons of literary theory, that I would end up taking from Baltimore when I left. Literary theory, after all, had begun to seem not so much like a profession as a luxury. As my thesis advisor often said, "I am rich, millions are not," quoting *American Psycho,* but he could just as well have been describing Johns Hopkins, an island of money in the midst of an alternately warring and desolate city that wasn't so much a twentieth-century relic as a window onto the twenty-first century.

As if to occupy us while we all waited for news that something had happened somewhere, in 2004, Mark Zuckerberg released a technology that hit Hopkins and spread quickly across campus like iPods had the year before. It was called The Facebook then and I discovered it while sipping coffee at the campus cafe above the underground library. A couple of students sitting at the table next to me, who sported the Hopkins uniform of North Face jacket and sweatpants, spoke excitedly of the new network and what they were able to see on the site. "Everyone's on it," they said, "you can see where they're from, where they live, and who their friends are. I don't know if it's creepy or cool."

I opened my clunky white iBook, typed www.thefacebook .com in the browser address bar, and created an account with my university email address. (This was required to log into Facebook then; one had to be a student at an Ivy or near–Ivy League school to use it.) It was true, you could see everything: all the students on campus, their pictures, their interests, their friends. And, in being able to see everything, I saw that The Facebook had miraculously solved the biggest social problem that plagued Hopkins and had led to its low rankings in student satisfaction. The campus had no public space aside from the library, which is why that afternoon, like most, I was sitting in the sunlit cafe with my laptop, taking a break from the dungeonlike stacks below. In an instant, Facebook had created a public space, albeit a virtual one, that was accessible at any time, from anywhere.

In 2004, other online social networks, like Friendster, already existed. However, most college students had spent their high school years on AOL, and knew that having a public, guileless, and unprotected Internet presence was little more than an invitation to be spammed by sexual solicitations from faraway men. Before social networks, AOL Instant Messenger and similar chat services were the only truly interactive, in-real-time forms of communication on the Web. In those days, I was always somewhat dismissive of boys who asked me if I had AIM, because it was obvious that they wanted to communicate in instant message form to avoid all the social challenges and filters of real life and, say, ask me out without having to look me in the eye, or look at me at all. So, the idea of creating a profile on an open, national social network felt like an unnecessary risk, another way of making yourself available to millions of distant strangers for the benefit of only a few friends. Who needed that? The lonely, maybe, or the exhibitionist, but most people weren't enough of either to make a public online profile listing all your private details that compelling. However, by building a virtual agora made up only of people you might actually know in real life, Facebook had suddenly created a good reason for everyone, not just the Internet-obsessed boy in his bedroom, to be identifiably on the Internet.

As one such boy who attended a class for which I served as a teaching assistant protested, pre-Facebook, and after Googling me without success, "You're not on the Internet!" (Because for the boy in his bedroom, and eventually for everyone else on the Internet, gathering data about people using Google felt like a god-given right). "Good," I replied, with satisfaction.

It wasn't like I didn't use the Internet, to the contrary. In the 1990s, when the Internet was in its infancy, I had an email account that I could only access using a no frills program that had no buttons like those currently seen on the Web; to send an email, I had to type a command like "send." Teenage hacker friends that I met at punk rock shows in Arizona used the Internet primarily to trade information about what were then high-tech hacks: a tone dialer cobbled together from Radio Shack gadgets that allowed you to make free phone calls from pay phones, or a breakdown of how credit-card numbers are generated that allowed you to crack credit cards. It almost seemed, then, that this was what the Internet was for: an anarchistic sphere devoted to wielding technology against corporations. I thought it was cool, but in the absence of sites targeted to more general interests there wasn't much for me to do online except write emails and visit bulletin boards, all green text on black screens.

A hacker once taught me that, in Pine, the email software used before AOL came along, you could type commands like "finger" to see when someone had last checked their email. This was when I realized that, online, there was always a way to get more data: You just had to know how to go deeper into the code and know more than the average user about its obscure loopholes and commands.

After the boom of the late 1990s ushered in the consumer Internet, I became a regular on forums devoted to fashion and style, such as Makeup Alley, where women traded beauty and fashion information. Under pseudonyms, we discussed our lives, always protecting our personal details from prying eyes or search-engine crawlers. The overriding rule of the Internet was simple then: You could say whatever you wanted as long as you didn't say who you were. I also took care to avoid all the cheap-seeming websites, like the fledgling MySpace, which appeared to be founded on the idea of empty exhibitionism and populated by predatory men looking for pictures of women to devour and discard. I was on the Internet enough to know that in the few short years that broadband had been available, it had become easy for men to find images of women to use as a shallow substitute for sex or love. For women, there was no value—there was even potential harm—in putting yourself online and offering yourself up to strangers, to have your image distributed infinitely across the Web. As the boys of the Internet often said on the troll-filled message board called the Daily Jolt, the only community discussion forum at Hopkins before Facebook landed, "There are no girls on the Internet." It was true; there weren't. If we were there, we were as protected by pseudonyms and secrecy as the guys who were searching for us.

Now, in the fall of 2004, with my newly created Facebook account, here I was: on the Internet under my real name. Visiting Facebook's rudimentary privacy page, which had just a few drop-downs that offered options to make your profile visible either only to your school or only to your friends, I realized that it was possible, for the first time on the Internet, to protect my profile from being visible to anyone outside of my immediate group of acquaintances. I breathed an elated sigh of relief. *Now, we can all finally use the Internet!* I thought. No more dealing with creepy guys assuming that just because I was on the Internet, I was available to be virtually stalked and harassed with pictures of penises, followed by a barrage of insults if I didn't respond. The privacy protections of the restricted network (people outside of Hopkins couldn't see my profile or even that I had one) made it feel, surprisingly, okay.

Facebook made it easy for the Internet-wary to be comfortable, because, in addition to the privacy protections, the initial layout of the site was minimalist to the extreme. It was strikingly clean, and novel in its simplicity, lacking the gaudy advertisements and spammy content that were inevitable elsewhere on the Internet. The profile consisted only of a modestly sized photo and a set of profile fields that the user could fill out or not, according to their own comfort level. It seemed fun, literary almost, like a newly published, frequently updating book that was more interesting to peruse than the dry, archaic texts I studied in the library. The first interest I listed on my profile was the *gold standard,* because I had always been interested in the idea of things that don't change form, that hold value, that aren't subject entirely to the whims of an economy in which nearly everything is disposable, temporary. The other interests I listed on my profile were flirtier and less abstract: *praias* ("beaches," in Portuguese), braiding my hair. This was the trick with Facebook, like the way you present yourself at a party: to say something without saying too much, to appear interesting without trying too hard, to be true to yourself without telling everyone everything. "Never apologize, never explain," Roland Barthes wrote in *The Pleasure of the Text,* which we studied in class. This seemed like the right way to approach a prying technology that, I could already sense, would never be satisfied by just a few bits of data. Much later, Facebook would seem to whisper, "Tell us everything." Even though in the beginning it was less inquisitive and shared your information less far afield, I already sensed that I had to remain its boss: I had to be able to tell it *no.*

Facebook was entertaining and engaging precisely because, unlike most technical applications at the time, it didn't seem like a sterile bunch of lines of code. Just as at the other prestigious universities that had Facebook networks, the Johns Hopkins University Facebook network was a delightful web of in-jokes about campus culture—such as the "I Check

Myself Out In The Mattin Center Windows" group devoted to the vanity-provoking windows of the Arts Center, or the "Hopkins 500," devoted to the approximately five hundred students who could be seen at parties interspersed with profile photos of artificially tanned sorority girls, intense medical students, and Hopkins' requisite lacrosse players. It was the first Internet site I had ever used that mirrored a real-life community. The cliques on Facebook were the same ones I ran into at the library and campus bar, and the things people said to each other on their walls—water polo team slang, hints at the past weekend's conquests, jabs at Hopkins' lacrosse archrival Duke—were similar to what you heard them saying at study tables or around pitchers of beer. The virtual space mapped the human space, and it had all happened virally in weeks.

Logging on to Facebook that first day, in retrospect, was the second, and to date the last, time that any technology has captured my imagination. The first was when Apple advertised the first laptop, the PowerBook, in the 1990s—with the words, "What's on your PowerBook?"

"World domination," my teenaged self answered instinctively. That's what these devices were made for, I thought: so small and yet so powerful, so capable of linking quickly to and between everything else in the world. I had a sudden fantasy of me, in ponytail and sweatshirt, remotely manipulating the world from a laptop, armed with ideas about how the world should be and the new ability to distribute them. From the laptop, I could write and distribute information faster than ever before. It was intoxicating to imagine, and Facebook's sudden, faithful rendering in 2004 of the physical world into the virtual felt the same. What could you do, now that you could see and connect to everyone and everything, instantly?

But what, also, could be diminished by such quick access? In the realm of ideas, it seemed easy: Who wouldn't want to distribute and discuss ideas widely? However, in the realm of the personal, it seemed more complicated. What was the benefit of doing everything in public? Were there types of information that made sense to distribute person to person and mouth to mouth, rather than digital page to digital page? Is information itself neutral, or do different types of information have different values, different levels of expectation of privacy, different implications for distribution and consumption? Did I *want* or *need* to know, passively and without asking or being told, who went out and what they wore and who hooked up the weekend before? Should all information be shared equally quickly and without regard to my relationship to it? And, finally, and most important, as we ask whenever we begin a new relationship with anything, would this be good for me?

Whether Facebook would be good for me in the long term was an open question, but in the immediate term it was, and rather quickly, to my surprise. It happened while I was perusing Facebook Groups, which I loved for their wealth of humorously delivered anthropological data. Reading them was much like being anthropologist Margaret Mead, but online, sitting on the couch in the comfort of pajamas and slippers. You could skip from the world of the lacrosse team to that of the small set of black Hopkins students, each with their own concerns and jokes and slang, in a span of seconds.

In this, Facebook Groups seemed more fun and less creepy than reading people's personal walls, which from the start had a slight, unseemly quality of eavesdropping on semiprivate, out-of-context, easy-to-misinterpret, conversations. The interjection of distant voices on friends' walls was always vaguely unreadable, unpredictable, illicit. "Let's play this weekend," a girl would post on the wall of a guy I knew, suggestively, and it felt weird to read, not because I didn't think girls liked him but because the utterance didn't actually reveal anything that was particularly relevant or useful. A girl wants him, I now knew, but I already knew that. Lots of girls did. The technology invited me to speculate about whether he wanted this girl back and whether they would go out and what would happen next, offline, all of which was really, in the end, irrelevant to be speculating on in advance. If two people like each other, they'll hook up, if not, they won't. All this noise was just noise, but a very present noise, a noise that we all, now, needed to consume, whether we cared to or not. In those cold November days, with the winter quickly coming on, there wasn't much else to do but watch and attend, curiously, to this new system that was just beginning, with a vengeance, to bring us online and publish the slightest social vicissitudes of our lives—the fact that someone likes us, the fact that we may be attending an event—to the world, for everyone to wonder about.

One such November day I discovered a group called "We're going to Brazil and you're not, bitches," referring to a Hopkins-led trip to Brazil that was happening a few weeks later. The group, like most Facebook statements that are about trumpeting some aspect of a person or group's identity, had no other purpose than to state that this group of students was going to Brazil and everyone else was not, bitches. My first thought was "Why didn't I know about this trip?" and then I recalled that without a public space outside of classrooms and the stacks, it was nearly impossible for Hopkins to distribute information about extracurricular activities. My second thought was, "I, too, am going on this trip, bitches." I mean, why not? I had nothing else to do.

I went straight to the campus study abroad office and asked them to put me on the Brazil trip, though it was only weeks away and they'd already processed everyone's visas and itineraries. Miraculously they did, and two weeks later I was on a flight to Rio de Janeiro, away from the academic dramas of the English department and into another, more vivacious society.

"You two are so California," our trip leader said one night in an outdoor bar in Brazil about me and a boy from Malibu wearing fluorescent sunglasses. He was a true California surfer kid, with a permanent tan and ocean-colored green eyes, and, in conversation, we discovered that we both dreamed idly of revolutions we wanted to play a part in someday. While the students from the East Coast gossiped about who had hooked up the night before, we talked about South American revolutionary movements that no one else on the trip had even heard of. This prompted them to perk up and listen. In the status hierarchy of the trip, we were California, and California was cool, and therefore revolutions were cool. "American culture starts in southern California and moves east," I always told people on the East Coast who wanted to know why I knew about something they didn't. This was before culture moved at lightning speed through the Internet, spreading from one coast to the other in minutes. I'm not sure now how anyone lays claim to cool anymore.

I wasn't actually from California, but people often made that mistake. I dressed with a casual beachiness and spoke with a slight Valley girl lilt that I never tried to lose. It was a hallmark that said (I hoped) that I didn't take myself too seriously. It took too much time to explain to people that before the real estate boom of the 2000s and its influx of midwesterners looking for a warm-weather McMansion, my home state of Arizona was like a bedroom community of San Diego, like southern California without the beach.

Being so close, and yet still a half-day's drive away from us, California was exciting, exotic, a dream of American perfection that we could actually touch. When school was out, my best friend Dana and I would drive the long desert highway to San Diego, entertaining ourselves by searching for the Hotel California, which legend said existed somewhere on the highway. "Is that it?" one of us would ask, upon seeing a white building silhouetted against the sky. "I don't know," the other would say, and we would drive on, searching. I think that we almost prayed that we would never find it, so that we could keep searching, forever.

When I returned to Hopkins I began the semester-long transition from my life as a graduate student to whatever would come next, which I didn't know yet. All I knew was that I had to leave the decaying east and find my way back west, to the place I belonged and where I had to believe, if only to ward off depression at my failed grad school career, that dreams still came true.

To this day, when I say "California," I usually mean the beach cities of the south, replete with surfers and sunshine, not the quasi-cosmopolitan north. Northern California is somewhere else, a California that was familiar to me in 2005 only from the Joan Didion essays that I devoured in my late teens, in search of life advice. "Q: In what way does the Holy Land resemble the Sacramento Valley? A: In the type and diversity of its agricultural products." Didion repeats, like her own accidental childhood mantra, and this always stuck in my head, a perfectly meaningless set of lines to someone who had never been to Sacramento, but suggestive of abundant riches tucked away somewhere north of Santa Barbara. It is perhaps because of this quote, and that I was broke, that I decided to move to northern California.

I ended up in Berkeley, which, with its large student population, was all I could afford. It was close enough to Silicon Valley, where I knew the money was, and was a much cheaper place to live than Palo Alto, where a one-bedroom apartment couldn't be had for less than $2000 a month. Through Craigslist, the 2005 unemployed person's best friend, I found an apartment near the university and a temporary job as a copywriter at a design firm in San Francisco. My job was to write copy for a line of skin-care products that were being manufactured as a house brand for Target. My initial enthusiasm quickly submerged by tedium, I wrote descriptions of cucumber-scented lotions and cleansers that I had never actually used. There were only so many ways to describe a face wash—invigorating, refreshing, cooling—and by the end of the month I felt like I had written all of them.

I was relieved at lunchtime when I could walk out of the office to San Francisco's long piers, enveloped by a perpetual fog that felt more like Oregon than California. Lunches at the aggressively artisanal cafes in the Ferry Building were too expensive for me, so I bought tacos from the Mexican food trucks that served the downtown's working class who commuted in, like me, from the East Bay.

Back in the design office, bored with the endless lines of copy that had all begun to sound the same, I would take to surfing Facebook. With very few features beyond profiles and messaging, Facebook was like a richer, more playful form of email, with the option to post public messages on people's walls. Since there weren't many fields, friends' posts occasionally had a deliberation and clarity that were entrancing, like you were reading little glimpses into the soul of the person—the thing they wanted most deeply to communicate to the world. Facebook was also a quick if not particularly satisfying salve for loneliness: In the Bay I knew no one, but online there were faces I knew, updating their pictures and profiles regularly, making familiar jokes.

In late July 2005, I had been working as a copywriter for a month when my boss, a micromanaging type with bleached teeth that glowed fluorescent, caught me looking at Facebook and chastised me. I felt indignant, given that in my view she was getting the most compelling descriptions of moisturizing cream that she could ask for from a random Craigslist hire. I even paid attention to alliteration and redundancy in my writing and fact-checked my work to make sure I wasn't making any overtly untrue claims about the ability of the products to make you more beautiful (and after doing this job I learned never to take any claims on a beauty product label seriously). But, as with many contract jobs, my work went largely unappreciated.

While I was illicitly perusing Facebook at work a few weeks later I noticed a bulletin on the normally blank homepage that said, "Do you want to work at Facebook? Send us your resume." That night I emailed my resume to the address listed, not knowing what they were looking for or what a job at Facebook might entail. I felt intrigued by the prospect, though. As new and strange a product as Facebook was, I sensed in it a power, the allure of a new social institution that had no limits and that might never end.

CHAPTER 1

WELCOME TO THE FACEBOOK

I don't know why Phil Rochester, who was engineering royalty in the valley and had been installed by venture capitalists to help with scaling up the tiny Facebook team, selected my resume from what must have been many that appeared in his inbox. I suspect that his choosing me had to do with the fact that Johns Hopkins featured prominently on my resume. He was a Vanderbilt alum, and I had learned in Baltimore that upper-crust southern elitism, conscious or not, runs deep. When I left Johns Hopkins, despite all its academic drama, my matriculation there faded immediately into a simple signifier of the elite. This is what an American private university is, not an education so much as a pedigree, a mark of distinction.

When Rochester called me he was at Costco buying tires,

multitasking with his BlackBerry in typical Silicon Valley fashion. He couldn't be bothered to conduct a proper interview. He assumed, efficiently, that as an English major from an elite school I was capable of answering user-support emails. "Come in Tuesday," he said. "You can try it for a few days. If you don't like it, you can leave. It pays twenty dollars an hour. That's pretty good, right?" he asked. "Uh, okay," I said. Neither the job nor the pay being offered was very good, but short of learning how to program, I knew couldn't compete for a real job in Silicon Valley. My only choice, if I was going to try to make my fortune there with all the others, was to find a way to make my lack of technical skill my strength.

Driving my scuffed white 1994 Camry into Palo Alto for the first time in early September 2005, I noticed instantly how perfectly bland and ordered the town was. The sidewalks off the main street were nearly as clean and prim as at Disneyland, or maybe, more aptly, *The Truman Show*. I had trouble finding the Facebook office at first ("It's up the stairs, at Emerson and University," Rochester had told me) and walked up the wrong set of stairs into a halfway house that operated in an old motel left over from the city's preboom days. That encounter with seediness would be my last in Palo Alto (the halfway house closed soon after and is now most likely a startup office).

"I don't even know what a quail looks like. . . . Facebook is hiring" was scrawled in chalk on a sandwich board at the foot of the stairs of the building next door, as if this was someone's boardwalk pizza parlor hiring for summer employees. I didn't know why they were talking about quails (I never did quite understand the reverence for quails or the fact that they showed up everywhere, on custom Facebook T-shirts and office white-boards, except that this was a private club and like any club it needed in-jokes), but the sign's irreverence was a relief: I might fit in here, I thought, in a way that I never had done in the hu-morless atmosphere of graduate school, which regarded all jokes as a suspect diversion from criticism.

As I entered through the office's glass doors I looked around for Mark Zuckerberg, whose name I knew only from the bottom of Facebook's pages, all of which read "A Mark Zuckerberg production." I imagined someone ghostly, dark haired, not unlike the half-blurry figure with mussed hair in the first Facebook logo (which turned out, disappointingly, to be a slightly modified piece of Microsoft clip art). He had to be dark to make something like this, I assumed. Facebook had too much gravitas already as a useful but slightly unnerving social experiment not to be created by someone with a streak of darkness.

It turned out that Mark preferred to work at night, I was told, when he had a home-court advantage over VCs and other businesspeople used to keeping regular daytime hours. I was surprised and not a little disappointed to find out when Mark finally came into the office later that day, preoccupied as always with taking calls and holding meetings behind the glass door of the video game room, that he was sandy blond, and not particu-larly tall. I imagined someone reedier, wilder looking, more dark genius in the basement than light-haired goofball in shorts and a Harvard hoodie, shuffling around in athletic shorts and Adidas sandals. We didn't actually meet on my first day: He reserved his hearty welcomes for the engineers, prodigal sons prized for their ability to convert life into lines of code. Customer support was barely on Mark's radar.

When I was finally introduced to Mark the following week, he smiled, seeming to like me well enough, although he soon moved brusquely to something else. He always seemed to be on a different plane when talking to nontechnical employees, distant and detached, reserving his attention for those who were directly important to him: VCs or his fellow founders, and then, gradually, the engineers that he took a liking to. It would take years for one of those people to be me. By then, people assumed that we were friends and had known each other forever. And I guess whether or not we were in fact lifelong friends was irrelevant, because, in the world we were making, all it took to establish a friendship was a few lines of code and a click of the friend button. I received a friend request from Mark a few days after our first meeting, and I clicked accept, though nothing particularly friendly had thus far transpired between us. But I was starting to see that, here, it didn't matter: The world of relationships, as far as Facebook is concerned, is simple.

At eleven in the morning on my first day at Facebook, the office was an empty warren of desks, about forty feet by forty, cluttered with open drink bottles, half-unwrapped snacks, and video games. A few desks were occupied by young, plain-looking guys in T-shirts, gazing at their screens. They looked barely awake, having not yet consumed their daily quota of bottled Starbucks coffee drinks and Red Bull and seemed startled, if not displeased, to see a strange new woman in the office. The only other woman in the office—an administrative assistant—was more animated, smiling toothily as she welcomed me in. She sat in front of a large piece of graffiti art featuring a cartoonish, heavy-breasted woman with green hair floating above an ominous cityscape, like an adolescent version of the eyeglasses over Gatsby's East Egg. Many of the pieces of graffiti in the room featured stylized women with large breasts bursting from small tops that tapered down to tiny waists, mimicking the proportions of female video game characters. It seemed juvenile, but I wasn't very bothered— it just seemed like the kind of thing suburban boys from Harvard would think was urban and cool.

"We had to move the really graphic painting to the men's bathroom because someone complained," an engineer told me as he gave me a tour of the tiny office. He said this with the slight mocking disapproval that was my new colleagues' default tone in response to anything that resisted their power. I got it: Just because a few women might be let into their Palo Alto clubhouse, we weren't supposed to complain about things like sexy images of women on the walls. This was their kingdom and their idea of cool, and we shouldn't mess with it. I could see that it was, in a sense, a test: If you couldn't handle the graffiti, or the unrepentantly boyish company culture it represented, the job wasn't going to work out. Easy, I thought, and anyway, given the absence of women around, I figured they would need me for something. You can't run a successful company with boys alone. The office was small but the stakes, I could tell, were already high. The cold, outsized confidence in the air—a sense of grim determination that accompanied the graffiti and the graphs and the scrawled in-jokes about quails on the whiteboards—said that they wanted to win it all.

Rochester eventually emerged from taking a phone call in

the kitchen. He was an august man with gray hair and an untucked faded polo, whose gaze would only ever seem to fully focus when he was talking animatedly to other engineers in the office about *scaling,* or keeping the site up in the face of increasing users and page views. Scaling, I would soon find out, was the fetish of the valley, something that engineers could and did talk about for hours. Things were either *scalable,* which meant they could help the site grow fast indefinitely, or *unscalable,* which meant that the offending feature had to be quickly excised or cancelled, because it would not lead to great, automated speed and size. Unscalable usually meant something, like personal contact with customers, that couldn't be automated, a dim reminder of the pre-industrial era, of human labor that couldn't be programmed away.

Though I didn't quite realize it on this first day at Facebook, I was in possession of a skill set—that of the English major—that was woefully unscalable as far as Facebook was concerned, more of a liability than an asset. When I perused Mark's profile on Facebook after we had become virtual friends, I noticed that in the Favorite Books field he wrote, "I don't read." Okay, I thought, gearing up for a long battle to be appreciated in my new role, this job *might* work out in the end but it is not going to be as easy as I had first thought.

Rochester's mature appearance made me think that perhaps this wasn't just the nerdiest fraternity house in Silicon Valley and that there might be some adults at the helm who understood the importance of having employees with different skill sets. He gathered me and Oliver, a blond Stanford poly-sci grad, into the conference room to give us a polite but rushed description of our new position. "You'll basically be answering emails from users. Jake will teach you how to do everything," he said, handing us off to Jake, another Stanford grad who had started as the first customer-support rep three weeks before. Now that we were here, he was our de facto manager, at least until the official customer support manager could be hired. I sensed from the glowing, familiar way that Rochester said Jake's name that they already considered him an old hand. When Jake walked into the room a few minutes later wearing a Stanford T-shirt and cargo shorts over a wiry, athletic frame, I guessed that their acceptance of him had to do with his classically preppy looks, like an Abercrombie model come to life. Facebook, it seemed, wanted to have it all: to be the new and scrappy kid on the block and also have the feel of an old boys' club that had been around forever.

"What email address do you want?" said a blond IT guy with a goofy smile that put me at ease, as he set me up on my new, work-supplied iBook. "Kate@facebook.com," I said immediately. He pushed the laptop over me so I could set my password. "It has to be strong," he said with a French accent, "that means it can't be an obvious word, and it needs special characters." I typed in a strong version of the word "Salvador," after my favorite city in Brazil, with a dollar sign instead of an "S." Maybe this technology will save us from something (loneliness, alienation, boredom—I wasn't sure), I thought, and if it doesn't, maybe it will at least save me, by making me some money and relieving me from the fate of having to start over from scratch, somewhere else, again. I was tired of starting over.

Launching my email program and seeing that "kate@face book.com" was my address was a heady feeling, like starting a new country in which I was the only Kate there, queen of a world in which every other Kate would be derived from my archetype. Facebook still had fewer than 5 million users, but I was sitting at the top of what would become a very large virtual land mass. Facebook's name alone gave me gut confidence in the site: It was a real-life term that represented the website's function exactly. In choosing this name, Mark had announced his intention not to create some type of Internet fad but to replicate a real world need for a basic human directory. Internet fads come and go, but directories—like phone books before everyone went mobile—satisfy the basic human need to find and stay in contact with people.

Jake, Oliver, and I huddled around the conference table with our laptops and some Cokes from the fridge, which Rochester had showed us proudly was stacked full with every caffeinated soda we could desire. The lights in the conference room were turned off, as Rochester assumed that, like the engineers, we would want the room to be as dark as possible. I always liked working in darkness; it made things feel more exciting, less like an office and more like we were peering out at the world on our screens from inside a cave. Jake introduced us to the janky application through which users' emails to Facebook flowed. Once we learned how the software worked, Jake taught us, without batting an eyelid, the master password by which we could log in as any Facebook user and access all their messages and data. "You can't write it down," he said, and so we committed it to memory, just the first of many secrets and customs we would learn as we became indoctrinated into our new lives as Internet social administrators.

I experienced a brief moment of stunned disbelief: They just hand over the password with no background check to make sure I am not a crazed stalker? I kept checking Jake's face to see if he would test or caution me in any way about how and how not to use the password, but he didn't. I worried I would be like a bull stepping into the proverbial china shop: What if I accidentally perform the data equivalent of knocking something over, accidentally changing someone's password or forgetting to log out of their account, posting on their profile when I meant to post on mine? As surprising as it was, in a way, it was also reassuring, a vote of confidence in me as I stepped into a vast sea of personal data.

Security measures would later be implemented that made it impossible for anyone to use the master password without authenticating themselves as an employee, and a year after that, the password would disappear entirely in favor of other, more secure forms of logging in to repair accounts. But, at the beginning, there was only one password, and like all the boys in the office, I now had the keys to the kingdom. The dummy account we logged into to administer each school network, equipped with a pixelated photo of Mark wearing an Oxford button-down and a slight smirk, was called "The Creator," and it did feel a bit like being a kind of omnipotent, all-seeing god.

After an hour's instruction from Jake, we were set loose on the emails flowing in from colleges across the United States. They ranged from the briefest request for a password to long expositions on the social phenomenon that was Facebook and the way it had already changed social interaction on campuses for better or for worse, depending on the author's viewpoint.

The most glowing fan letters to Facebook betrayed the author's new sense of power while using this technology: even the shyest person could now glean information and participate virtually in social worlds that formerly seemed restricted or off limits.

There were also complaints about the usual stalker types familiar from the rest of the Internet, voraciously devouring images of women, seeking the most flesh-baring photographs, and spamming women with requests for sex. Jake, Oliver, and I played the police of the virtual college campus, issuing warnings and adjudicating arguments, and were also its tour guides, explaining how poking and tagging and blocking worked to people who were just learning to conceive their social lives in virtual terms.

"What does poking mean?" was a question asked hundreds of times a day, sometimes by people who really didn't know and other times by people who relished the sexual frisson of writing to Facebook to ask about "poking" and its many interpretations. We always responded innocently, "It's just a way to get someone's attention," knowing full well the range of childish and sexual connotations in play. Being coy, not admitting the libidinal urges driving so much of the site's usage, was professionally necessary, a way to differentiate Facebook from the cheap and overtly sexual vibes of MySpace. Being coy was also part of the fun, part of the illusion we as a company were constructing that life on Facebook, unlike in reality, was always safe, easy, playful, free, void of cost or obligation. As Dustin Moskovitz, Mark's Harvard roommate and Facebook co-founder, said over lunch in the office that fall, with his dry, practical intelligence, "Everything on Facebook is flirty." He was right. Facebook, like flirting, was a fun way to present yourself lightly and attractively to the world, with no downside, and no commitment.

A few weeks later, just as I was beginning to worry that I would be one of the only women working at Facebook, Maryann and Emma joined the customer support team. They were close friends of Jake and Oliver's from Stanford, pleasant in appearance, also nontechnical in major, and we got along as well as needed to perform our duties. At night they disappeared to parties full of former Stanford students and the requisite ping-pong balls and beer-laden Beirut (beer pong) tables that were their university's preferred nighttime sport.

This particular social clique preferred to discuss parties to more personal or intellectual topics, so we didn't go beyond casual pleasantries, but that was fitting for our mission of superficially connecting everyone in the world. We had Facebook as a topic of conversation. If we wanted to know more about each other we could visit each other's profiles and read the details we put there, and if we wanted to get closer than that, we could IM each other privately. From my first day onward, it was like my coworkers and I were connected always, virtually at least, chatting and emailing and posting on each other's Facebook walls. The first thing Dustin said to me after I had been taught my initial Facebook duties was to get on AIM. "We are on it all the time," he said, and it was true, for better or worse, we were.

Since a formal coolness was how our team interacted— smiling nods followed by fast descent into our screens and the emails and Facebook pages contained therein—users were my most emotionally expressive correspondents that fall. Thousands of emails flooded our system each day asking us for everything from just letting them in because they didn't have a college email address to solving their messiest social problems, asking if we could delete a regretted message before someone read it or let them see the account of someone who had blocked them. The angst that flowed through onto my screen was overwhelming, sometimes. I felt a bit like the advice columnist Dear Abby for a digital age, counseling people on various online social minefields and talking them down from ledges. Facebook made it so easy to say things that people said things they regretted, and as I read the distraught emails I started to feel an apprehension. What happens to society when you promise people they can have whatever they want: instant contact, hundreds of photographs of people you barely know, endless digital validation? Real life has limits, but the Internet, where everything seems free for the taking, has none. What will this do to our relationships, I wondered, or even more intimately, our souls?

For us, as administrators, everything on Facebook really was there for the seeing, as we were not subjected to the privacy barriers that existed for regular users. Our tools displayed everything that happened on the network: last logins, location of login, and deleted posts. We even had an internal tool, called appropriately, Facebook Stalker, that showed who had looked at our profile, which revealed fascinating insights. For one, my female friends studied my profile more often and for longer periods of time than my male friends, which suggests a digital version of the old dictum that women dress for each other, not for men. With access to every piece of data that existed on the system, working at Facebook was like playing the game from the hacker's side, despite the fact that I wasn't a hacker: The users gave us data freely and we consumed it, delighting in the new facts that came in by the hour.

As exhausting as answering emails for eight hours a day could get, there was something rich and fertile about Facebook as both company and product that was seductive, enticing. This is something that could go on forever, I thought, not like a business but like a family, like royalty, like the Dallas oil scene of Silicon Valley, crowning its own kings and queens and generating its own society. Who wouldn't want to be a part of that?

On Friday afternoons we got together for All Hands meetings. I looked forward to them because they were the one time we discussed things as a company, and the only meetings when everyone at the company was included. Mark would stand somewhere in the office, his posture unusually straight for someone dressed casually in a joke T-shirt (around this time he preferred one that said "I love Sloths") and sandals. Everyone would gather round, sitting on desks with flip-flops dangling or on the floor with legs crossed, watching and listening while Mark discussed the week's business: deals made, products launched, technical issues experienced and resolved. Occasionally, Matt Cohler, a Yale guy with a VC background, would chime in on financial things or Dustin would comment on site growth and health and any major down time that week. Everyone watched in rapt attention, smiling, as there was much to smile about: We had so much to do, together, and the All Hands were where we got our motivation for the next week and months.

As we worked steadily in October 2005 to prepare for the launch of the Facebook Photos feature, where users would finally be able to upload photo albums to their profiles (prior to the launch of Photos, the only photo a user could post was their profile photo), Mark referred to all of us in an All Hands meeting as a "Facebook family," and even though most of us had just met, the kinship was palpable. It also would be profitable for us to get along; if we liked and cared for each other, it would be easier to accomplish the high goals Mark was setting out for us: more Facebook networks, more Facebook features, an ever-faster flow of information.

I liked to listen to Mark's discussion of the product philosophy and goals at these meetings, which were to me the most fascinating part of the job: what were we trying to do, with this fledgling Internet identity registration system? "I just want to create information flow," he said in his still nearly adolescent voice, lips pursed forward as if jumping to the next word, and everyone would nod, all cogitating in their own way about what this meant. Mark's idea of information flow, though vague, was also too vague to be disagreed with, and even if we came up with counter-instances to a model of pure information efficiency (for example, I wondered, do I want my Social Security number to flow freely?), we knew that we weren't supposed to disagree. Mark was our leader, for better or worse. When the meetings ended he would say either "domination" or "revolution," with a joking flourish of a fist, and everyone would laugh, nervously, but with a warm and almost chilling excitement. It was like we were being given a charter, by a boy younger than most of us, to take over the world and get paid to do it.

Aside from the general questions that I started to ponder, questions such as what were we were doing, and what did it all mean, and that I kept to myself, there was one area of our work in Customer Support that required us to have philosophical discussion and debate. Facebook, like the Internet in general, made it so easy for people to post and gain visibility for content that people with extreme and often unpopular views went wild on the new platform, creating groups devoted to whatever cause they espoused. Most of these groups were devoted to bullying of some kind, from petty harassment of a classmate to hatred of a marginalized group.

In the Customer Support Team's daily discussions of what behavior would be permitted on Facebook, we decided that any attack on an individual person would be against our Terms of Service, since we had no interest in or ability to track down the validity of any bullying claims. How were we to know why some woman on campus was being called "a slut" or "whore"—the common bullying claims made against female Facebook users— and why would we care to investigate such invidious claims? Further, individuals were the core users of the service, so to allow for the bullying of individuals would hurt the product's growth, and for us, growth was paramount. People had to have a basic sense of safety while using Facebook if they were going to use it at all.

Attacks on groups of people were harder to interpret and

police, since it was difficult to tell when something was hate speech, free speech, a political disagreement or some combination thereof. (Was the group "I hate people who wear Crocs" hate speech? We had to consider it, along with the more serious hate groups aimed at blacks and gays.) Many Facebook groups made it easy for us to decide: They posted pictures of dead and gored bodies and were covered in swastikas and death threats. In the odd logic of our work, it was almost a relief to see blatant death threats because they meant that we didn't have to comb the group looking for indications of the creator's intent (people on the Internet are rarely subtle in their hatred). Thus, after long discussion we decided that if a group contained any threat of violence against a person or persons, it would be removed. One aspect of our jobs, then, became scanning group descriptions for evidence of death threats, and searching for pictures of dead people. This was the dark side of the social network, the opposite of the party photos with smiling college kids and their plastic cups of beer, and we saw it every day.

One afternoon, as I sat on the couch in the office reading emails, a user at a school in the Midwest wrote in to report a group that was devoted to gay bashing. Upon investigating the group I found that it indeed violated the Facebook terms of "no death threats," as the words "kill gays" were all over the page. With a click of a button in my administrative tool, the group was deleted. I also wrote an email to let the offending group creator know that his hate speech wouldn't be tolerated. This commenced a long correspondence between me and this unfortunate soul in the heartland who insisted, virulently, upon his right to say anything he chose about gays. He also baited me by creating new groups with increasingly violent slogans and images of beheaded bodies, which I continued to delete, responding as calmly as I could. Finally, just as I was fearing that this stalemate would go on forever, I happened to glance at his password, which in the early days was displayed next to a user's name in our admin tool. "Ilovejason," it said. Pitying him more than feeling angry, I wrote back and told him that this case was closed and if he created one more hate group I would disable his Facebook account forever. He stopped writing after that.

Between the alternately dull and dramatic emails from users, the highlight of the work week was Friday afternoon happy hour, when at around five o'clock, our caterer would wheel a table laden with snacks, wine, and beer directly into the grid of desks where we sat. Engineers would emerge from behind their screens for a few minutes to grab a beer and return as quickly as possible to their screens. Customer support employees, who were hourly rather than salaried workers, would continue to dash off emails to users, sometimes with a beer in hand, before clocking out and grabbing another beer and gathering on the gray, modern mass-market couches in an alcove near the office entrance to talk.

By six or seven o'clock, after a few beers, people grew chattier, engineers and admins and customer support reps mingled, and we began to get to know one another in person. It felt like that early moment in any social circle when you're not sure what will happen: Who will be friends with whom, what cliques will form, who will be most popular? It all still felt protean, unformed, like the first months of freshman year. All that was clear was that Mark was in charge, supported by a small group of deputies from Harvard and Yale—Dustin, Matt—and it was up to the rest of us to figure out what our roles would be and where we would fit.

Mark rarely drank or socialized at the happy hours with the rest of us. Occasionally I heard stories, sometimes from Mark himself, about parties and high jinks at the house in Palo Alto that he had lived in with Dustin and a few other engineers the year before—something about a drunken flight on a zip line and another story about blown circuitry in the middle of a beer-fueled coding session. There were whispers that they used Facebook to stalk Stanford girls and invite them to parties, but that made them no different than most guys on the network. But, by fall 2005, when I started working there, Mark's demeanor in the office, if it had ever been particularly relaxed, was already developing into that of the intent executive preoccupied with larger things than company happy hours, despite the fact that he wore shorts and T-shirts and often padded around the office barefoot.

The most relaxed I ever saw Mark was when my dad, a math professor, came to visit the office one happy hour that fall. Suddenly every engineer in the office, including a suddenly smiling and talkative Mark, gathered around my dad to talk about calculus and graphs. I hadn't even told anyone that my dad taught math; it was like they sensed a kindred, elder spirit, someone who understood with them that graphs were the most beautiful and inspiring things in the world. Mark was so at ease and unassuming in that conversation that when I asked my dad as we left the office, "What did you think of Mark?" he answered, "Which one was Mark?" I had the thought then, as we walked to dinner at the Italian place down the street, that it was my dad, and not me, who should be working at Facebook: Unlike me, he would instantly fit in, and everyone could talk about graphs happily ever after. But my dad didn't need a job, and I did, so my dad flew back to Phoenix and I stayed in Silicon Valley with the engineers and the graphs.

In the small office of twenty engineers and a smattering of support reps and admins who were rapidly becoming friends, Mark's presence tended to be more aloof than the others. He walked with his chest puffed out, Napoleon-style, his curly hair jumping forward from his forehead as if to announce him in advance. My general sense of camaraderie with most of the engineers, with whom I had exchanged at least a few words around the kitchen fridge or over a beer at happy hour, felt cooler in relation to Mark. Someone has to be the boss, and no one likes the boss (do they?) and so it seemed natural that I felt nothing more than a slight wariness around him, born of his Silicon Valley status as an anointed boy wonder. He seemed more of a necessary evil. I was almost relieved that he was so distant, so preoccupied—like a father you know won't be overly concerned about what you were up to.

Three weeks after I started working there, Facebook celebrated its five-millionth user by throwing a party in a dimly lit space below a swank new restaurant in San Francisco. It was the first and last company party I attended that was made up mostly of people—adults—who didn't work there. (As we grew bigger, we turned inward, populating parties mainly with Facebook employees, until it felt like we were our own island.) The five-millionth-user party was attended mostly by venture capitalists, curious or invested in this new, already buzzing upstart of a company. The name Peter Thiel, PayPal's infamous founder and billionaire, was on everyone's lips, but I couldn't identify him because all the men at the party looked like a version of him: dirty blond, excessively fit, with drinks held casually against their unbuttoned blazers as they discussed investment business and tried hard to impress one another. My customer support teammates and I stuck mostly to ourselves in the corner, having nothing to offer the investors, watching while they swarmed over the mussy-haired engineers standing around clutching barely touched drinks.

As I sat on a couch watching all this in my cocktail dress, holding a melting gin and tonic, I wondered at the VCs' obvious predilection for boys who looked like younger versions of themselves. I could see that as a woman I would automatically appear alien in this context. An engineer came by to take photographs and I posed, smiling, with my female teammates. One always had to smile and appear happy for Facebook. The photographer moved on to another group and I went back to musing.

It often felt like this at Facebook, like I was the only one who was watching, seeing what was happening not as a privileged participant but as an observer. Dustin, the most critically astute of the Facebook founders, did not fail to notice. A year after I started working there, we were talking at a smoke-filled party somewhere in the Stanford hills when he said to me, matter-of-factly, "You're going to write a book about us," as we descended the stairs into a crowded den to watch a band that had just begun to play.

CHAPTER 2

IN HACK WE TRUST

That first winter, to go along with the perks of meals, laundry, and gym memberships that Facebook provided, the company rented a house in Tahoe for employees to use on the weekends. Mark is serious about wanting us to have fun, I thought. The prospect of escaping my queue of Facebook user emails to frolic for a couple of days in the woods sounded ideal, but the three-hour drive to Tahoe and sixty-dollar-per-day ski resort tickets were more than I could afford on my customer support salary. I felt lucky and relieved every month just to make my thousand-dollar rent and my four-hundred-dollar student loan payment. Anything else was a rare, luxurious extra.

But Facebook, maybe more than any other company, was a social scene, and I knew that it would be important to take part in company social events whenever possible. When Luke, an engineer who had recently quit grad school at Stanford to work at Facebook, invited me and my customer support teammate Maryann to go to the Tahoe house in January with him, Dustin, and Mark, I was excited. It was a good crew, I thought. Luke surfed ocean waves in his spare time in addition to surfing the Internet at work, and was chiller than the typical engineer. He reminded me of someone you might chat with over beers at a beach bonfire while on vacation. Dustin, who, like Luke, was from Florida, was also fun and sociable when he wasn't sleepless and stressed from his responsibility of making sure that the site stayed up at all hours of the day and night. Maryann was a tall, beautiful woman from Stanford by way of Marin County, San Francisco's wealthy northern suburb. She had a perfect smile and never seemed to complain, and in this, she was, some of our colleagues remarked longingly, their ideal woman, wholesome and girlish. Maryann would eventually become the literal face of the company: her beatifically smiling picture appears to this day in the sample "Jane Smith" account that is used in Facebook's new feature announcements. Back then, however, Maryann and I were just among a few token female employees, similarly dressed in jeans, T-shirts, and long ponytails, recently embarked on what would be for both of us a long journey with the company.

After the drive to Tahoe, we threw our things on bunks, then gathered around the table to drink cheap Trader Joe's wine and listen to music. As the night proceeded and we became steadily more drunk, we played mp3s on someone's iPod louder and louder, screaming the lyrics to Green Day and

Sublime so loudly that we were essentially doing karaoke, the singers' voices drowned out. Sensing that this moment called for more entertainment, I donned the bearskin, complete with head, that adorned the banister on the stairs leading to Mark's and Dustin's rooms (like all companies, ours functioned according to status hierarchy; the important people got the best rooms while the rest of us slept on bunk beds downstairs). Mark thought this was hilarious and insisted that I continue to wear the bearskin around my shoulders. Luke, who built the wildly successful Facebook Photos product that had launched months before, naturally took pictures all night of our shenanigans to post to Facebook in an album he titled "Opening Night," so the rest of the company could see how much fun we were having.

In one of the last photos Luke took, Mark is gesturing at me haughtily like an emperor as I stand doubled over in laughter with the bear suit draped over me. It was all innocent fun; everyone was laughing and enjoying themselves, but when I saw the photograph appear in a Facebook album on Monday I was struck by the loaded nature of the image, ripe for interpretation, in which Mark appeared to be commanding an employee, female, to submit. If I were his PR person, I thought, I would tell Luke to take it down. Whether to protect the company, or Mark, or myself, I wasn't sure. In this take-no-prisoners company, where you were either willing to devote your whole young life to it or not, it was starting to be hard to tell the difference. I felt certain that some gossip writer was going to find the photo and post it in an article about Facebook someday. In fact, the photograph appeared in Gawker four years later, with the caption, "This one *also* might lead the confused and bewildered to conclude that Mark Zuckerberg got drunk in Lake Tahoe and taunted a co-worker."

Perhaps more interesting than the fact that the photo was taken and posted on Facebook is that it didn't occur to anyone in the office that there was anything wrong with it, or that the picture revealed something about the culture of Facebook that it shouldn't. Mark was too busy programming to get to the part of a liberal arts education where you study social inequality. As he wrote on his business card with boyish hubris, "I'm CEO, bitch." That image was saying that power wasn't something to be questioned; it was something to collect and brandish. This—not the anarchist ethos I knew from my punk-rock hacker friends— was Facebook's new world order.

As the months passed, moments like these occurred with unsettling regularity. When a female employee reported being told by a male coworker in the lunch line that her backside looked tasty—"I want to put my teeth in your ass," was what the coworker said—Mark asked at an All Hands (it was hard to tell whether it was with faux or genuine naiveté), "What does that even mean?" I went to Mark at the open office hour he kept after the meeting and told him that it was unacceptable to blow off sexual harassment in the office. He listened to me, which I appreciated, but understanding of the crux of the matter; that is, that women by virtue of our low rank and small numbers were already in a vulnerable situation in the office, did not seem to register.

Confronting him that day simply had the effect, I think, not of making him more sympathetic to women's plight at Facebook, but of making him realize that I was a force he would have to reckon with. Employees weren't supposed to challenge his power, but when we did we became, paradoxically, the thing we were supposed to be in the action-hero logic of the company: a rule-breaker, a threat, and, therefore, someone of interest to be courted and co-opted.

Mark's tendency to mock or disregard everything that wasn't a technical issue triggered a sinking feeling that accompanied the heady glee we all began to feel over the early months and years as the Web site soared higher and higher, gaining more users and more rounds of funding and more celebrity. Sometimes my head spun just thinking about it—the wealth, the power, the eventual fame for all these people, I could see it all happening. This is the American dream, I thought, wide-eyed, for who even believed in the American dream anymore? In grad school we invoked the Horatio Alger myth to discredit any ideological move that was designed to distract the masses by suggesting that anyone could be rich, anyone could succeed. The irony of being a critic of the Horatio Alger myth only to end up in my own Horatio Alger narrative was almost too much.

I was a student of the humanities, including histories of colonialism and revolutions and, despite Mark's talk in All Hands, I knew that the war that Facebook was waging, if it continued the way it was going, wasn't exactly revolutionary. The company's entire human-resources architecture (and, conveniently, Facebook had no actual HR department to correct any of this for a long time) was constructed on the reactionary model of an office from the 1950s, in which men with so-called masculine qualities (being technical, breaking things, moving fast) were idealized as brilliant and visionary while everyone else (particularly the nontechnical employees on the customer-support team, who were mostly female and sometimes, unlike the white and Asian engineering team, black) were assumed to be duller, incapable of quick and intelligent thought. It was like *Mad Men* but real and happening in the current moment, as if in repudiation of fifty years of social progress.

For example, on Mark's birthday, in May 2006, I received an email from his administrative assistant telling me that it would be my job that day, along with all the other women in the office, to wear a T-shirt with Mark's picture on it. Wait, what? I thought, *he's not my god or my president; I just work here.* The men in the office were told that they would be wearing Adidas sandals that day, also in homage to Mark. The gender coding was clear: women were to declare allegiance to Mark, and men were to become Mark, or to at least dress like him. I decided that this was more than I could stomach and stayed home to play sick that day. I was the only one. The other women in the office, including Mark's girlfriend, who did not work at Facebook, but had come to the office to celebrate his birthday, happily posed for pictures wearing identical shirts printed with Mark's picture, like teenage girls at an *NSYNC concert or more disturbingly, like so many polygamous wives in a cult. These pictures also appeared in Gawker years later, making me relieved that I had stayed home so that I wasn't immortalized forever online in such a strange, *Stepford-Wives*-like pose. I wondered if any of the women had been secretly troubled by the request that they pay homage to Mark or if, as often seemed the case, everyone was just happy to belong to something.

My customer-support teammates, like Maryann, were always cheerful and pleasant, but having been friends since their freshman year, they were naturally much closer to one another than they were to me. Maryann and Jake soon seemed to be dating, though, being cagey as Facebook employees often were, they didn't make it Facebook official for years (they would eventually, like many of our colleagues, become engaged). I wondered if I would ever have my own clique at the company. It seemed important: people to post on your wall, to invite you to events, to pose with you in photographs at company parties.

In January 2006, a new engineer showed up. We struck up a conversation at happy hour that, to my delight and surprise, veered away from the usual topics of Facebook administrative duties and programming issues. "In my interview, Luke told me I could work on studying gender dynamics on Facebook by looking at the data sets," Sam said, "and that's one of my main interests, so I decided to come to work here." (Once hired, he was assigned to product development rather than, as had been advertised, to research.) He wore an old, tattered D.A.R.E T-shirt from the 1990s, baggy, unpretentious jeans like a skateboarder, had alert eyes and an impish smile. In other words, he was exactly the type of guy I was friends with—a little indie, cute, not obsessed with polish—but also, openly gay. This was unusual at Facebook and, I realized as we chattered on about topics of great interest to both of us, like gender studies and the futility of grad school (he had been contemplating grad school prior to being offered the Facebook job), a welcome development. By the end of the night, after most customer support team members had gone home and Mark and a few engineers were still staring at their screens in the back of the office, Sam and I were trading quotes from the movie *Heathers*. "Lunchtime poll," one of us said, and we both delivered the line from the movie in unison. "Aliens land on the earth and say they are going to blow it up in three days. But the same day you get a call from Publishers Clearing House saying you've won five million dollars. What do you do?" we recited with mock *Heathers*-like haughtiness that dissolved in laughter. That night when I left the office, for the first time since setting foot there, I felt elated, like everything was going to be okay, because I finally had a real friend at Facebook.

Sam and I weren't the only ones obsessed with movies. Mark and Dustin kept quoting from their favorite action flicks, like *Top Gun,* on the footers of pages of the site, such as "Too close for missiles, I'm switching to guns." This wasn't just a job or a website or even a social network, the quotes seemed to be saying that it was war, and it needed to feel and look like one, complete with battles waged and won, soldiers bloodied and triumphant, camaraderie formed, just like in the movies.

Perhaps this really was what Mark was thinking. He seemed not so much to be on a mission for programmers, but for heroes, protagonists, leading men. That spring, Mark brought in five engineers from Harvard who became known as the Microsoft Five, after the old-guard software company in Seattle where some had previously worked. The Microsoft Five sounded like some kind of cowboy band who rides into town and shoots up a saloon in a Western.

As the Silicon Valley legend goes, the Five received their Facebook job offers while at a party. Their first reaction, allegedly, was to reject the offer. They assumed that the upstart Facebook couldn't pay them enough or treat them as seriously as they were accustomed to being treated. The Five's initial disinterest gave Facebook the drive to wage one of the first of many oedipal raids on an older company's talent, in which Mark could prove that despite the company's youth and scrappiness it could win the brawl for status. It seemed sometimes that, to Mark, battling a bigger competitor was almost as exciting as winning the war, as I would see again when, three years later, we turned our attention to the valley's biggest behemoth, Google.

Once the Five had been convinced to come to Palo Alto, they immediately wore, without flinching, the new label *star programmer,* not just a coder but a personality, a social leader, a celebrity center around which the valley's attention can swirl. Jamie, who, unlike the other four, came from Amazon but was included in the Five, was the clear prize for this new celebrity model of Silicon Valley; he was tall, dark blond, handsome, and of very old money. He looked like a gentleman in the nineteenth-century portraits that hung on the wall in my seminar room at Hopkins. The other four guys weren't as portrait-perfect as Jamie; they looked less like movie stars and unlike him, had not been the presidents of painfully elite Harvard final clubs, replete with invitation-only parties and secret rituals. However, in the race for status that Facebook was mounting, they had enough: They were from Harvard and they were programmers, which made them the valley's version of good old boys. The Microsoft Five quickly established themselves as a new, explicit kind of fraternity: They called themselves Tau Phi Beta, or TFB for The Facebook Fraternity, complete with Greek letters, custom T-shirts, and weekly keg parties at the house they rented together.

Sitting there in the office in my usual uniform of worn jeans and cardigan, watching this new social order unfold, I felt that, as they say in Internet speak, we were doing it wrong. While having an office social scene was necessary, nobody really likes fraternities, with their macho attitude, hazing rituals, and beer-soaked party aftermaths. If we were supposed to be cool and California, calmly convincing people that it was okay to pass us their most private data on a daily basis, we would have to come across as less aggravatingly aggressive than a fraternity house.

Bringing employees together, in the life-as-work-and-work-as-life culture of late 2000s Silicon Valley, was a core business mission of any startup. It wasn't enough to work there, you had to devote as much of your life to it as possible. At Facebook, being a startup devoted to virtual socializing, we couldn't just work all the time. We had to have some kind of scene in which human stories could unfold, if only in the first instance to have something to document on Facebook. We needed to entertain each other.

This seemed to be part of the motivation behind the company's various social perks, such as the happy hours, catered lunches and dinners, regularly occurring company parties (in which employees were bused to a venue, provided copious amounts of liquor, and photographed by professionals hired for the occasion), and the houses that had sprung up, such as TFB (the Facebook fraternity) and the house in Tahoe.

As the site's user base nearly doubled throughout that spring, from 5.5 million users to ten, and everyone's sense of responsibility magnified by the week, I had the idea, selfishly perhaps, that a pool house would be a better way to lighten up and bring us closer than a frat house. After all, what better way to establish good cheer and team spirit than around a pool, drinks in hand, sun shimmering off the water? "We should get a house with a pool," I said to Mark one night that spring during the Friday happy hour. He flashed his characteristic look of askance approval, smiling, but looking half-away, as if to retain his sense of executive control. "That's a good idea," he said, pulling out his BlackBerry (huge by today's standards) to dash off an email with the request.

I was stoked about the pool house. At that point in my life, I was in need of two things: an outlet for my revolutionary energy and a new career that would work out in a way that grad school had not. Throwing my entire lot in with Facebook (to the point, even, of moving in with my coworkers at a company pool house) could turn out to be perfect. My interest in the Hotel California had not faded a bit since the days when my friend Dana and I drove the highway to San Diego searching for it. What more perfect metaphor for American society, and its obsession with belonging, with scenes of darkness and excess, with cults that you fall into and find it hard to leave? It felt like America was right there with me, ripe for a new experiment in community spirit. And the pool house would be my Hotel California.

As we were moving into the summer house in Menlo Park, I placed a Hotel California LP on the mantel in the empty living room. I smiled to myself as I regarded it sitting there, with its picture of a classic Los Angeles hotel illuminated golden behind palms, unnoticed by my colleagues milling around the house. In addition to the record and my clothes, all I brought to the house that day were a few books that I'd packed to help me make sense of this new scene about which I knew little. Joan Didion's famous words from *Slouching Towards Bethlehem* were on my mind that afternoon as the sun set on our new house and I settled my things into my room. "California is a place in which a boom mentality and a sense of Chekhovian loss meet in uneasy suspension; in which the mind is troubled by some buried but ineradicable suspicion that things better work here, because here, beneath the immense bleached sky, is where we run out of continent." We, I felt that day, was me, a conglomerate of one, at the end of a line and the beginning of another, staking a claim to what I suspected would be a new gold rush.

Unlike the office with its domineering male energy, the house felt relaxed and cool, I thought with satisfaction, as I toured it in a denim skirt and flip-flops. A seventies ranch home of no architectural value, the house was solid—a little better, as most things are, for the wear and tear. The front yard sported *Edward Scissorhands*-like topiary bushes and a perfectly green lawn. As is typical in suburbia, the front living room sat in shadow behind closed drapes and went largely unused. The back den with the requisite seventies-porn-movie-style wet bar, stone fireplace, and sliding glass door to the pool, was where we would socialize. It was a little like being in *The Brady Bunch,* without parents.

Mark's room was across from mine, small and bare, but he didn't stay there. He had a famously minimalist apartment nearby (he claimed to own no furniture and have only a mattress on the floor for a bed) but he kept the room as a social placeholder, coming over with his friends or his girlfriend on the evenings and weekends to hang out. When he was at the house he invariably took up position under a Roman-looking tent by the pool, pacing back and forth while he mulled over the day's business. In his sandals and shorts, with his hand sometimes raised to his chin while he mused, he looked every bit the part of a little emperor.

I remarked on this to Sam as we lay in our bathing suits on the pool deck that first weekend, surveying the scene. Since meeting at happy hour, we had quickly formed something of an alliance. Alone, we might just have been the odd employees interested in something besides accumulating mountains of data and power but, together, we were the weird kids who occupied the far edge of Facebook's cultural map, composed mainly of Harvard fraternity boys, preppy Stanford kids, and other engineers of similar provenance. Sam and I claimed the pool as our de facto territory, given that we were more comfortable in swimsuits and in the sun than most of the engineers, and set up our towels on the deck in the afternoons to watch the goings on around the house.

Lucy, a petite, good-natured Stanford ex-cheerleader who had recently been added to the customer-support team, lived at the house and often worked on answering emails from the pool, her laptop perched precariously on the edge of the deck. Fiercely competitive (she made sure to win all sports competitions held at Facebook, like the yearly Game Day, which wasn't very hard to do, considering that most employees weren't particularly athletic), she made it a point to answer more emails than anyone else, even while half submersed in the pool in a bikini and turning a deep tan.

Maryann also often came to the pool in her bikini and set up her towel nearby, tanning quietly behind big sunglasses, pleasant and reserved as always. She was unequivocally considered hot at the company. But, I sensed, the last thing you wanted at Facebook was to be the hot girl, especially if you weren't protected, as Maryann was, by a close group of college friends who also worked there.

One day, one of the sales guys told me pointedly that I was hot, reminding me that I was surrounded by men who were in the habit of sorting women into hot or not-hot categories. Facemash, Mark's first website at Harvard, was designed to allow viewers to rank the attractiveness of Harvard students' photos. I wanted to be the cool girl, not the hot girl. The cool girl always has a chance of winning, because she has something beyond looks. As Stevie Nicks once said about her trip through the male-dominated music business, "I never wanted to be too pretty."

At another summer barbecue, I overheard Mark talking with some engineers about whether it was better to date a girl for looks or intelligence. "I dated a model once who was really hot, but my girlfriend is actually smart," he said, as if they were mutually exclusive categories. "Why can't a girl be pretty and smart?" I asked him in front of everyone. "Why does it have to be one or the other?" The group went quiet for a second, seeming confused. I knew then that if you had to pick one in order to succeed at Facebook, smart, not hot, was the thing to be.

On weekend afternoons, there were usually some boys milling about the pool house with laptops or beers drawn from a keg that was kept under Mark's tent. Occasionally someone important—usually an exec or VC, who would pull up to the house in a blaze of Audi exhaust—came over to talk to Mark in hushed tones under the tent. "It feels like we are in ancient Greece," I observed to Sam. There was not much for us to do at the pool house, though I found out later that, while he was pacing and we were sunning, one of the things Mark was mulling was whether to sell the company to Yahoo! for one billion dollars. I had a vague sense from the intense vibes during those days that something very serious was under consideration, but I didn't think for a minute that Mark might sell the company and we'd all cash out and go home so soon: We had a pool house, a gathering mass of enthusiastic boys (and a few equally energetic girls), and the future to dominate.

One newcomer, who claimed a room on the opposite end of the shag-carpeted hall from mine, struck me as another kindred spirit like Sam, though at first I had no idea why. Tall and lanky, he didn't have any visible muscle, just long boyish limbs. His face was pale and his hair paler, his eyes close together and set far back, hidden by a coy bowl of dishwater blond hair. I felt strangely, incongruously sure of him, having the unbidden thought as we talked by the pool on our first night in the house that he had a good heart.

My sense was that he brought a mysterious form of light, some spirit that we were all seeking, to the house. His name was Thrax.

A few months earlier, I was working at the office when someone sitting at a nearby desk said, "We've been hacked." I looked over his shoulder at a Facebook account they were eyeing. It looked like a MySpace page. That is, all the profile owner's information was perfectly arrayed as they had entered it on Facebook, but the formatting had been tricked into rendering like MySpace, with shouting features of gaudy colors, floating text, and smarmy profile fields like "Mood" and "Who I'd Like to Meet."

Dustin worked quickly to trace the hack to its source while the rest of us looked on at our screens in puzzlement. When he found the hack, or perhaps when it had found him (the whole point of hacking is not so much to break something as to get attention for breaking something, and so a hacker is not likely to rest long without telling someone, often the hacked, about the exploit), he told us the hacker's name. Curious, I looked up his profile.

My first reaction to Thrax's profile picture, of a bony college kid in an American Apparel T-shirt and a mop of emo hair, with red paint Photoshopped over his lips for effect, was that this kid wants attention so bad it's painful. He looked like the kind of wiseass who wants to make you pay. For what, it didn't matter.

At the time of the hack, Thrax lived in Georgia, attending a Southern college most of us had never heard of. However, he wouldn't live in obscurity for much longer: Dustin hired him a few weeks later, on the theory that you want to keep your enemies close, especially when they can break your site. So, a few days later, Thrax showed up in the office, wearing the same skinny T-shirt and baggy jeans he had worn on his Facebook profile.

From the minute he arrived, despite or maybe in part because of his cagey, impudent gaze beneath his long bangs, there was an almost preternatural aura of celebrity and inevitability about Thrax: The Harvard guys, who had made careers doing everything by the book, had been looking for this boy, long before they knew that this hacker savant from Georgia actually existed. At happy hour on Thrax's first day in the office, everyone swarmed him, asking questions about the hack and about his strange provenance in a state far from all of our own. A few of the Harvard engineers, perhaps miffed that they would now have to share the spotlight, wondered if Thrax was just a *script kiddie,* a derogatory term for an unschooled kid who copies code from the Internet rather than composing it himself. From my vantage point in the office, watching, I felt a sense of bemused relief. Things are finally going to get interesting. The Harvard boys have some competition, and Thrax seemed to understand, if nothing else, how to create a mysterious, compelling character out of the bits of the Internet that he mastered with his oddly long, ghostly white fingers.

Facebook was waiting for Thrax and brethren to arrive because, unlike startups that build computer chips or enterprise software, the network is about two things: personality and stories. People and stories are what keep us coming to the site. Whether out of an instinctive need to keep tabs on our surroundings or as a way of fostering social bonds, it is human nature to want to know what is happening to the people in our circle and, with Facebook, we don't have to bother to ask them. But, like any novel or film, a story requires characters and drama.

The Harvard boys couldn't satisfy this need alone. Their knowledge of the Internet derived from books and computer science coursework, not the trolling, rule-free websites where kids from the middle of nowhere honed their understanding of Internet warfare and developed well-known online profiles and networks of like-minded hacker friends. One of these friends, Emile, had worked with Thrax remotely (they lived in different states at the time) on the hack and, after Thrax arrived and was a hit at Facebook, the Harvard engineers tracked him down in Louisiana and asked him down to the office. When Emile showed up for his interview, it was the first time that Thrax, along with everyone else, had met him in real life. After some hand-wringing by the Harvard guys about whether any or all of these unschooled hacker boys from the middle of nowhere were just script kiddies, Emile was hired on, too. I liked Emile: Underneath all his trolling and half-shaved, half-long metal haircut, he too, I sensed, had a good heart.

Indeed, the hacker's appeal for the valley's legions of software engineers, business development execs, and money guys is not in what he makes (most hacks are by definition, technically shoddy, because they are executed quickly) but in the fact that you never know what he is going to do, what boundaries he will transgress. Silicon Valley imagines that the hacker's moves are sylphlike, quick, and made under the cover of night, while rule-abiding citizens, powerless, are asleep. In short, the hacker is sexy, a dangerous, bad-boy version of the plain programmer at work in his cubicle. The hacker's capacity to surprise—or in Silicon Valley parlance, *disrupt*—is fetishized in the valley as a source of power and profit for tech companies, Facebook among them, which considers its stated ability to "move fast and break things" a core company value. As Paul Graham, the valley's revered hacker guru and founder of the prestigious seed-capital firm YCombinator, put it while lecturing to valley entrepreneurs at what is called *Startup School,* "We don't want people who do what they are told." Or, as the startup enthusiasts on Graham's Hacker News board counsel each other, "It is better to ask for forgiveness than permission."

As Facebook matured, the staff came to encompass three distinct types of guys. Skilled, dependable programmers, often Asian-American or foreign born, who were hired to code and keep the site running. Supervising them, the Harvard and Stanford boys, mostly white, who wrote code, while they acted as the reassuringly familiar white faces of the company and ascended the ranks into leadership positions. Finally, the elusive, heavily video recorded, highly sought-after hackers, whose job was as much to act the part of the fresh-faced rogue impresario as to write code. Facebook needed these three types because while all could code, the hacker was what the quiet programmers and by-the-books college boys couldn't be: the classic, renegade American hero that we all know from books and movies.

It was a hot July afternoon in the office and I was being barraged with IM's from colleagues asking me if I was dating Sam. These were people who didn't usually IM me; they were the office social hubs, usually Harvard and Stanford guys, who felt it was their job to stay on top of all relevant office gossip that may affect the company social scene. There were lots of office couples developing, and so they wanted to make sure they stayed up to date on the latest romantic news.

"Huh?" I typed back to the many queries. "Sam is gay. Didn't you know that?"

"Yeah, but it says on Facebook that you guys are complicated."

"What?"

I went to Facebook and saw that on my profile I was suddenly "in a complicated relationship with Samuel Henley," and there was even a story to that effect: "July 23, 2 AM: Kate Losse and Samuel Henley are in a complicated relationship." Oh, I thought, I get it. Sam was testing the new product, News Feed, which would launch weeks later. Engineers and customer support were always testing as part of our preparation for product launches, trying to find the bugs in a feature before launch, and around the office testing was a good occasion for a joke on everyone else. We could get away with anything if we said it was a test.

Still, I was taken aback by the fact that the site had literally written a story about us and distributed it to our friends, illustrated with a photograph that had been posted to Facebook a few weeks earlier, of Sam and me in the pool at the summer house. This fully articulated story, written and illustrated by a machine, meant that authorship was no longer human but algorithmic; we didn't write our own stories anymore. In the photograph the algorithm chose to illustrate our new relationship (to provide visuals for a relationship story, News Feed finds a photo in which both parties to the new relationship have been tagged), we were dangling over the edge of the summer-house pool, our bodies trailing off into the water, and Sam was smiling straight into the camera, while I look slightly off center, quizzical. The water was a beautiful green, pacific, surrounded by darkness. It was an entrancing picture and I could see why everyone, regardless of the fact that Sam and I were just friends, wanted the story to be true. Everyone loves love stories, even if they are just the byproduct of a quality assurance test.

This new product was intended, as all engineering innovations are, to produce efficiency, allowing us to consume content about our friends more easily and automatically than before. However, the publicity provided by News Feed, the way it functioned like a newspaper, did more than just feed information more efficiently. It established a world in which anything that happened to us became food for a narrative, in which we became like characters in a novel that Facebook and its algorithms were writing, whether we wanted to be in it or not.

As was the case with all new features, we had already been using News Feed for months before it launched. As I lay around the pool house with my laptop, watching people play, I was also reading the newspaper-style updates that would appear in my feed. They were usually photo albums from fellow coworkers— pictures of parties at the summer house and elsewhere around Palo Alto.

The general concept of News Feed was simple: An algorithm was now surfacing content that it believed, based on your activity on the site (what you looked at), you would find interesting. But like all technology, the social news generated by a computer lacked some of the nuance of the real-life gossip channels it replicated. Information that would have gotten to you via human contact and conversation now surfaced as impersonally as if you were reading the *New York Times* (or more aptly, *People*).

As News Feed was nearing completion in August 2006, I was sitting on the gray modern couches in a sunny alcove on the engineering floor, testing the feature, when Pasha, the product manager in charge of News Feed and the only woman with an engineering background at Facebook, asked me to review some of the stories for wording. "I'm not good at this," she said, "You are. Help me." I supposed that she had turned to me because at that point I had already developed a reputation as the literary one, due to my status updates composed of music and literary quotes and my general disinterest in saying anything absolutely literal.

Pasha handed me a printout of the News Feed stories the team had prepared. At first glance they were, technically, neat: pulling profile photos and updates from the story's characters to create an algorithmically generated story. However, as I read through them I cringed a bit—they were not about telling a meaningful story, they were about delivering news in as hard and fast a way as possible. "So and so is no longer in a relationship," the story said, illustrating the news with an icon of a broken heart, one not unlike the icon of a broken hard drive that signals doom on an old Macintosh. Building the algorithm was one thing, I realized, but delivering stories that felt like they had been delivered by a human was another. I tried to intuit what model of the social world the stories assumed, and if it was one I recognized. Some of the stories didn't seem like anything I would be instantly apprised of in real life: For example, that some acquaintances were having a party I wasn't invited to, or that an old ex-boyfriend was now in a new relationship. While in real life I might find out about these things later, they just weren't things that I needed or wanted to know immediately, as they happened.

I shared my concerns about the bluntness of News Feed with Pasha—that it wasn't just telling me things quickly but telling me things I typically wouldn't know about—and she said that she would take them back to the engineers. None of the stories were removed. I wondered, then, if News Feed and the future of Facebook would be built on the model of how social cohesion works—what is comfortable and relevant to you and what isn't—or if it would be indifferent to etiquette and sensitivity. It turned out to be the latter, and I'm not sure Mark knew the difference. To him and many of the engineers, it seemed, more data is always good, regardless of how you get it. Social graces—and privacy and psychological well-being, for that matter—are just obstacles in the way of having more information.

As I worked with my fellow Customer Support Team members to help engineers test News Feed and work out the bugs, I began to see that we were trafficking in a new kind of programmed, automatic gossip, in which the mere act of updating your profile (or in this case, of Sam updating his profile and linking to me) becomes a story—online and off. The machine becomes the wandering bard, telling stories, real or something other. As Jean Baudrillard wrote, "The map becomes the territory."

When Sam was done testing a few days later, he removed our relationship from the site and we went back to being single, to the disappointment of our coworkers. And in the meantime, News Feed slowly became the core of the Facebook product, occupying the center of the homepage and, increasingly, the center of our social lives.

In a sense, Thrax's Facebook hack in spring 2006, which, in addition to making Facebook look like MySpace, also generated innocuous conversation posted to unsuspecting users' walls (e.g., "Hey, nice shoes," or, "This wall is now about trains.") was the first to elide our speech, motivated by individual intention, with that of a machine's. Unlike the usual viruses that create spammy posts that are trying to sell something, Thrax's Facebook worm created conversational messages that sounded like posts a friend might have written. "The whole point of them was that they could have been real," Thrax explained, describing the hack later to an adoring tech blogger. I doubt, however, that making a philosophical point was the hack's main goal, as Thrax and the other hacker boys that came to Facebook rarely trafficked in philosophical arguments. They preferred instead to use the Internet to create and distribute as many "lulz," or jokes, as possible. Lulz, on the Internet, were a goal in themselves, a new way of creating a scene and attracting attention from people waiting patiently to be entertained in front of their screens.

Thrax's Facebook hack was just the latest in a long sequence of virtual scenes that he had made. He told me about them as we hung around the pool house that summer, tapping away on our laptops at the kitchen table or strumming on guitars in the dark on the living room couches. As a child, his mother arranged for him to have headshots taken and shopped him around at auditions for child actors. When that didn't pan out, he took to the online world, where he and his friends created online personas and held LAN parties (in which people network some computers together in a room and play games) late into the night.

In high school, Thrax built a website (ready-made blog sites like Tumblr and WordPress didn't exist yet) where he blogged about the parties he went to each weekend. "Everyone at my school read it," he recalled. "There was always drama on Monday about what I had written and everyone would talk about it all week." By college, he was an active participant in the Something Awful forums, a site where people who are essentially professional Internet users (though they were often only thirteen years old) stay abreast of every meme and Internet in-joke cresting through the online world.

People in forums like Something Awful and the infamous 4Chan—an anonymous message board with a no-rules policy that results in an endless contest by users to shock one another with the disturbing or merely absurd—don't use the Internet the same way average Internet users do. They play the Internet like a war. The goal is to win every battle—a comment war, an attack against a Web page, or a contest to create the funniest memes. Battle is waged by an often passive-aggressive, often humorous Internet kind of fighting called *trolling*, and the best troll wins. The trick of trolling is to prove that you know more than your opponent—via wit, argument, or sometimes, silence—to show that they don't control you. In Internet culture, everyone is either the king or the pawn—or what, in Internet culture circa 2006, was "the pwned," a combination of "pawned" and "owned" that means both.

One Saturday afternoon that summer, as we lounged on couches in the pool house, half surfing our laptops and half talking, sometimes sending AIM messages though we were sitting three feet away from each other, Thrax told me a story from his precollege years. One day, Something Awful's moderators decided that, finally, he'd gone too far with his trolling and banished him from the site. To Thrax, this was worse than a very public high-school breakup. "That's when I realized how much of an asshole I was," he recalled, with a seriousness that verged on what almost seemed like tears, "It really affected me and I felt devastated." As I listened to Thrax talk about the dark days of his ban, slightly confused by the amount of emotion he felt for his banished Internet profile, I perceived a new, strange kind of existential crisis that affected these young men: a failure to exist virtually.

That summer, I dismissed this insight. Thrax was simply an interesting kind of freak and there would never be a mainstream market for his brand of obsessive online self-documentation and attention-seeking. I was wrong.

It was ten o'clock on a weeknight in July and the streets of Menlo Park were, as usual, dark and empty. Thrax and I were driving to Safeway to buy groceries. The radio in his car, a used BMW that he had bought off of Craigslist a few weeks earlier for six thousand in cash, worked intermittently, and received just one signal from an old-timey jazz station that only played at night. These technical limitations, rare in a world where engineers could deploy technology to get whatever they wanted, already felt like they fostered a kind of luxury, a rare form of value. Instead of choosing from ten GBs of pirated, curated, and sorted mp3s, we were grasping to pull one radio signal from the air, and it would play what it chose, in analog.

There were two Safeways in Menlo Park. A new one, with soft tones and Whole Foods–like stage lighting, and an old one, with seventies signage and the harsh glare of fluorescents. The old one was scheduled to be torn down but, for the time being, it stayed open twenty-four hours, so we always ended up there. We went grocery shopping in the middle of the night because it was the only time that we were both awake. In the morning, Thrax was sleeping and I would be at work. After midnight, he was working (or at least he was at the office, where he alternately coded, watched, or filmed videos, and managed his Internet presence across multiple forums and sites) and I would be asleep. Our schedules overlapped only between ten and midnight, and this is when we became friends.

In the empty Safeway lot, Thrax parked his car, letting the jazz station that we fought so hard to find trail on for a few seconds before turning off the engine. As we walked toward the fluorescence of the grocery store, I noticed that we were both wearing thrift store T-shirts and old jeans: the suburban indie uniform, though we both come from places the other has never been. I was surprised that we had anything in common at all, not just our clothes, but music, our dry humor. Georgia seemed too far to be familiar. I'd read too many stories about the South in my literature classes to think of it as anything but other: a place where all the American themes of racial darkness twist into something even darker, stranger, more impenetrable than in the American states like California and Connecticut, which are seemingly without accent. Yet here we were in the parking lot in the middle of the night, two young Americans on a mission to buy groceries in matching outfits.

Though we were in California, Thrax's grocery list read like it was definitely from somewhere else. Bologna, white bread, Miracle Whip. We wandered the overly bright, unkempt deli side of the decaying Safeway for fifteen minutes looking for sale bologna, meaning that it cost ten cents less than the one that wasn't. Thrax explained that in Georgia he was able to eat for twenty dollars a week just by buying the right bologna. This confused me, because he was earning at least twice what I was, and even I couldn't imagine that the five or ten cents' difference mattered. But he was strangely resolute about buying the cheapest sandwich ingredients.

As I followed him around the aisles, I found this to be equal parts cute, as if he were introducing me to his former life as a scrappy, d.i.y. Georgia teenager, and equal parts a sign of the telltale deployment of power that marks the powerful. Driving a used BMW to Safeway to buy the cheapest sandwich ingredients to save the pennies, the constantly weighing pleasure versus cost, was all part of the game, of the calculation required to organize the resources to build the things that would remake the world the way it should be.

Eventually we found the cheapest bologna, bread, and spread. Thrax was incensed that even the budget bologna was at least thirty cents more than it was in Georgia and complained about it all the way to the produce section. Once we were there, he forgot all about the bologna and started making fun of me for looking for organic fruit. I could see why the idea of organic produce was ridiculous to him; he didn't eat it, as it was never on sale at whatever Georgia supermarkets he bought his bologna from in college. He couldn't know that it tasted better than the genetically manipulated fruit sold at Walmart, and so, of course, the whole idea of organic seemed like some kind of Ponzi scheme that only a naive California girl would fall for.

This is the classic position of the nineteen-year-old boy hacker: He thinks that, by having nothing and being from nowhere, he can outsmart everyone and build an empire without anyone taking notice. He thinks everyone is by definition an easy mark, comparatively weak, because he assumes they have it better than him. He thinks he will know, unlike the naive masses, when he's being taken for a ride. His job—which is also his identity, an identity he chose at around age thirteen when he first began searching the Internet for evidence of how it worked, of how it could be broken—is to find the holes, whether in a website or in someone's logic, that he can exploit.

That night in the grocery store I could have tried to explain to Thrax, but didn't, that I bought organic food because it makes me feel better, and that this was my hack: to live as richly as possible with next to nothing, with few reliable career prospects as of yet, in a place that didn't have as ready and profitable a place for me as it did for him. I invested in what made me feel sharpest, most lithe, most radiant for the long term, because I knew that if I was going to pull off this hack, it was going to take a while. In that sense, perhaps it wasn't a hack, but then neither would his be. We were both going to use Facebook to get what we wanted. We loved Facebook—it had already given us information, power—and we knew it would use us, too, so we felt that it was fair. Hackers, like everyone else, have a morality of sorts.

Most of the men in the office, at twenty-three or twenty-four, were too old and too formally educated to qualify as authentic, self-made hackers, but everyone wanted to imagine himself as one. So, that summer, Mark ensured that the new office—now at 156 University Avenue, after we outgrew the first one—was decorated as a kind of shrine to the boy king. The top floor, which was allocated to nonengineers because it was too sunny to suit the tastes of engineers, was plain and relatively clean, lit by large windows that revealed the perennially blue Palo Alto sky.

The engineering floor below was dim, with blinds drawn, and decorated in cool tones of gray under all the empty drink bottles, shipping boxes, and candy wrappers that collected amid twenty-four-hour coding sessions. Desks were squeezed in like a battalion, from the entrance hallway all the way to the back of the room, where Mark's desk sat clean and bare, furnished only with his laptop. The other engineers' desks were piled high with toys and gadgets and screens: At least one thirty-inch monitor and several extra smaller screens just in case (we customer-support reps were each given one twenty-four-inch monitor). A set of TV screens mounted all along one wall displayed graphs depicting various site statistics: egress and active users and the current load on the servers. Occasionally, like in any fraternity house or other place where young men gather, the men on the engineering floor would play pranks on one another by putting embarrassing photographs of each other on the screens for all to view.

The floor wasn't all young men: By the summer of 2006, three women held product manager positions in engineering. All had been friends with at least one of the early engineers before they were hired. To become a product manager, it seemed, you had to be vetted as much for your ability to get along with the guys as for your product management skills, so no women were ever hired cold into this role. The PMs were a welcome, necessary presence on the floor, providing a warmer reception when customer-support employees occasionally went down to the E-floor, as the engineering floor was called, to discuss preparations for upcoming Facebook features. The men were friendly on an individual basis, too, but the overall atmosphere of the engineering floor tended toward the tense and aggressive. One of the Harvard guys was always jokingly threatening other engineers that he would punch them in the face if they displeased him, until even the most combative engineers had had enough of his violent banter and asked him to cut it out. Regardless, humor around the office usually had a warring, masculine bent, which came from the top: "Domination," Mark was always saying, joking in a way that was also, you knew, serious.

There were also often moments of levity during the workday in those early months. One afternoon, as we sat on the third floor answering emails, Maryann got an IM from the floor below that said that we needed to come downstairs quickly to see something. "What's happening," I wondered, as we got up from our desks and walked down to E. The boys—nineteen-year-old designer Justin, who had been recently convinced to drop out of college and come to work at Facebook, Thrax, and anyone else with hair that was long enough to flip out of his face at the end of a faux runway—were in the midst of doing a fashion walkoff, starting at one end of the office and walking like runway models to the other side as engineers and customer-support team members cheered them on. They pretended to flip blazers over their shoulders like so many *GQ* models.

At the far end of the engineering floor were two small rooms that served as the war rooms, where engineers could work intensely together on developing new products. To the left was Mark's office, a spare white room straight out of a mafia interrogation scene. The room to the right was where the boys would hide out and sometimes build things they weren't supposed to: It was piled with screens and blankets, as if they were living and sleeping inside the screen. Large letters spelling "Lockdown" hung on the door, declaring a state of product emergency even when there wasn't one. The engineers seemed to like the idea of a perpetual lockdown because, on such occasions, they were expected to spend all their time in the office, focused fully on the mission. Between the rooms was a couch piled with more blankets, oddly cozy and comfortable, from which one could survey the whole floor. When I walked the gantlet of desks to get to the end of the office, which I had to do occasionally when I came down from the top floor for meetings, I was relieved to get to the couch, away from the prying eyes following me and to a place where I could turn my gaze on them. In its architecture, both virtual and physical, Facebook was like one big battle to retain control of the gaze.

The mere fact that we worked in an office presented a structural issue to overcome: Real hackers don't work in offices. They work at home, in their parents' basements, or anywhere but an established work environment. After the move to the new office, Thrax told me about a time in college when he and a friend drove to New York City to visit their Internet forum friends and ran low on cash. In order to afford the gas to drive back to Georgia, he pulled over to the side of the road, his friend took out his laptop, found an open wifi signal, and hacked into the AAA Web site to get a discount for gas in order to get them home. Hacking, like any other rogue American pursuit, abhors the corporate in favor of the casual or even slightly illicit, which is why Mark hired graffiti artist David Choe to paint the walls of Facebook offices with scheming figures holding their fists high.

To make sure the engineering floor felt as playful and casual as possible, it was decorated with toys of all kinds: scooters, deejay equipment, Lego sets, puzzles. Every once in a while, Dustin would order a particularly interesting and expensive toy online to entertain the engineers and have it delivered to the office. One day that summer, a lifelike dinosaur that somehow grows arrived in the mail. Everyone cooed over the new robot pet and took photos of it to upload to Facebook. Another day, a king's crown—replete with fake jewels and red velvet—materialized, and the boys took turns trying it on. It settled, finally, on Thrax, who by virtue of his age and unschooled pedigree was the true boy king. The crown eventually became the prototype for one of the first virtual gifts that Facebook would sell, and naturally the gifts' first buyers were the engineers, who took turns buying each other virtual crowns to post on each other's walls.

Looking like you are playing, even when you are working, was a key part of the aesthetic, a way for Facebook to differentiate itself from the companies it wants to divert young employees from and a way to make everything seem, always, like a game. In the ideology of the new Silicon Valley, work was for the owned. Play was for the owners. There was a fundamental capitalism at work: While they abhorred the idea of being a wage slave, the young men of Silicon Valley were not trying to tear down the capitalist system. They were trying to become its new masters.

Without anything academic to study in Palo Alto, I kept myself entertained by studying people. By day, I studied the profiles of the people whose Facebook accounts I had to log in to and fix or investigate. I developed a taxonomy of all the different types of college users. There were surprisingly few types: the fraternity kids, the artsy alternative kids, the middle-of-the-road boys and girls who play soccer and study political science. My favorite profiles, more often than not, were those of black students, who tended to use Facebook more socially and conversationally than white students. It reminded me of a difference I had observed in Baltimore between the anxious, solitary white grad students and friendlier, more talkative local Baltimoreans, making me wonder if black culture, or maybe just southern culture, placed more emphasis on community and conversation, whereas white culture was focused more on the idea of every man for him or herself.

Around this period, we discovered a bug that affected the inboxes of people with over five hundred messages. They would suddenly see a so-called ghost message hovering in their inbox. As soon as someone wrote in to report the bug, I knew that, most likely, they were black. White people, I discovered by reading people's messages and walls, tended to lurk and judge more than they communicated, so their accounts rarely generated that bug. It was almost as if the system itself was designed for lurking instead of direct communication and broke under any different mode of use.

By night, in Menlo Park, I studied the engineers as they came over to the pool house to grill, swim, and socialize. They were always a little anxious and awkward, working to remain calm and in control in situations where their programs weren't at hand to do that for them. When all else failed, we could always talk about the site, because it consumed our days, transacting almost all of our activities and experiences. It seemed like we wrote on each other's walls as much as we saw each other in person. And also, we each had a life-changing financial interest in making the site as addictive and ubiquitous as possible.

It felt somehow life-affirming to be away from the computer, to see people in person instead of reading their intensely crafted profiles on Facebook. I had already started to wonder whether the fact that I was more comfortable offline than on, unlike the engineers, would mean that I would have to be the bearer of the human—the one who feels where others couldn't or wouldn't.

I kept a running tally in my head of the things and activities in the summer house that seemed human and normal, looking for reassuring evidence that, despite Facebook's fascination with the cool, technical mediation of our lives we were just warm, social animals after all. I used what I knew of life from Baltimore as my gauge. Baltimore is maybe the least technically advanced, most tragically human place in America. Kids in Baltimore didn't hack or have computers; hacking for them meant hanging wires from window to window to poach electricity from the house across the way. I kept Baltimore's poverty in mind as the baseline against which all this Silicon Valley technology and all the real-life fantasy it enables could be measured.

On weekends, the house's dining room table was converted to a Beirut (beer pong) table for parties, and I counted this as a positive: Beirut was clearly active, social, real. At Hopkins we played it in dirty row-house fraternity basements that were the privileged mirror of the dirty row houses that the poor squatted in only streets away. I gave the Beirut table extra points for being a little messy, a little loud, a little burly (involving cheap beer rather than smooth, pricey liquor), and because laptops weren't safe there amid the flying ping-pong balls and splashing beer. Anything that got engineers off their computers must be healthy.

People brought instruments to the house and played them, and this too seemed like a reassuring sign. Mark had a guitar and on occasion he played Green Day songs while we all sang. Pictures of these sing-alongs also made their way to Gawker three years later, but the bloggers didn't find the video on Facebook of us singing "Wonderwall" and its rousing chorus of "Mayyyybe, you're gonna be the one that saves meeeeeeeee." I sang extra loud on the chorus, perhaps aware of the lyrics' special resonance. Watching the video again on Facebook today, I noticed that we seemed much happier here than in later videos, brimming with energies that have long since been focused and contained.

I suppose that that summer, nothing was certain; it all could have turned out to be an odd camp that we attended and then disbanded, instead of an early moment of youthful alacrity in a company's inexorable rise to power.

Thrax kept a stock of musical instruments in the den that he played whenever there was anyone to listen, and he had a crowd-pleasing ability to instantly play any song he had ever heard. At parties, he entertained guests by playing songs on the keyboard long into the night. Thrax's total lyrical recall intrigued me from the first, seeming like the musical expression of all the autistic savant tendencies of Silicon Valley, a way of turning all their obsessive, numerical perfectionism into music. Eventually it came to seem, like the emerging social Internet itself, to be just another way of grabbing and keeping attention, of saying, "Look at me." But, for a while, it was entertaining, even charming, a gift of song in a sterile valley.

One night, at two in the morning, as people gathered with their beers around Thrax's electric piano, I asked him to play "Hotel California." For once, he didn't know the words, so I had to sing them. The boys in the office preferred Daft Punk and the song "Robot Rock" as an anthem, speaking excitedly and without irony of wanting to become robots one day. That made me wonder: Why? What's the pull of being a robot? I imagined that being a robot sounded as unnatural to me as my obsession with Hotel California must have seemed to them. No one ever asked about the Hotel California record on the mantel or why I'd put it there. The record, like all of this, and like the viral memes we would be in the business of distributing, seemed to have just happened, part of an odd conglomeration of things and people that have convened here, now, to be grouped together for a while, only to later disperse.

"The site broke," someone yelled from the den after Thrax's off-key version of "Hotel California" had trailed off. The boys happily retreated to their laptops to log in and start fixing bugs. They always brought their MacBook Pros with them to parties, and they seemed happy to have an excuse to have their familiar screens in front of them, networked to the system and to distant friends on instant message. When the evening would take its usual, inevitable turn and morph into a laptop party (you could always count on something breaking back then— breaking and bringing the site back up at two in the morning was part of the glory), I would just shrug and go outside to the pool, alone. It wouldn't be my way to confront the boys about their antisocial-seeming commitment to technology, at least at first. In those early years, my stance toward the company and the new world we were creating remained anthropological and cautiously optimistic. I had some notion that a writer doesn't intervene in her subject until she feels she understands it. That summer, there were still a lot of unknowns to be reckoned with.

When the house wasn't swarmed by engineers and their laptops, it was cool, open, empty, mine. I liked to pad around the carpeted rooms, reflecting mostly on the fact that I was happy to be here, now. I was entranced by the deep stillness of Menlo Park, the light, fir-scented breeze that entered through the open windows at nightfall, the way the cool darkness seemed to aid both looking back and looking forward. I felt lucky to have the rich privilege of starting my life anew, with fifty or so smart people, in very fertile circumstances, though the payoff we were working for wouldn't manifest itself for a while. For now, the stillness—the absence of the sirens of Baltimore, the cool peace, the warm sense of limitless potential and profit—was enough.

CHAPTER 3

PIRATES OF THE RIVIERA

> You run, I con. A tiger don't change its stripes.—thrax96
> Huh?—k8che
> That's from *Lost*. I think I'm going to put that on my
> Facebook business card.—thrax96

When I first began working at Facebook and Dustin said, "Get on AIM, we're on it all the time," he wasn't joking. Most conversations in the office, from the driest work-related exchange to the most overt flirtation, happened on AIM. At times, this led to confusion—an engineering manager might send you an AIM asking you to go get coffee during work hours but it would be unclear whether this was for professional or personal reasons. At that moment he could be interested in befriending you, just as later he might be arranging your promotion. When you were online, with your Adium (our preferred AIM client) status set to available, it was open season in terms of what you might get in the way of messages: Because we were sitting at different desks and often in different rooms, separated and protected by technology, anything could happen and often did.

"Can you introduce me to that Japanese girl you are working with?" was one AIM message I received from an older database engineer who was known to exclusively date Japanese women. Having read Edward Said's *Orientalism,* like any liberal arts student, it was hard for me not to find this somewhat suspect. "Not right now, we're working," I thought, but simply pretended I didn't get the message. AIM, like the social Internet generally, was more about your desires than it was about social graces. Any messages you didn't want to answer, you could just pretend not to have seen it on your screen. Conversations faded in and out, rising and falling in intensity depending on the participants' interest, with an impunity that would be considered rude in real life.

I quickly learned to ignore most of the random messages from guys in the office—they were just sending out a quick ping to see if I was clueless enough to accept a date from someone who could easily be asking the same thing of twenty other girls at the same time. I paid attention to instant messages from Thrax, though, because we were friends. "I just saw that there's a shower room on the third floor that has shampoo and towels; it's well-equipped," I typed to Thrax at work one day and he answered, with a suggestive non sequitur, "Yes, yes, I am," and I thought, "Did he just say that at work? Are we awkward, hormonal teenagers or coworkers?" I guessed that, symbolically at least, we were both. Instant messaging, like everything we were building, was a way to play without consequences, the adult-proof playground of the digital age.

At the end of that first summer, the office was a focused hum of work, punctuated by the usual happy hours and periods of playtime. Engineers were preparing to launch News Feed in September, and in customer support we were doing our routine work of answering emails while also helping out with feedback and testing for the new feature. I had received a tiny promotion to senior customer-support rep and an even tinier raise, at fifty cents more than my previous hourly wage.

As we were getting ready to move out of the pool house, Thrax instant messaged me that he and Sam were going to Las Vegas for the yearly hacking convention called Defcon. "You can come if you want," he typed, and I did. Not just because I liked them and our indie-ish little crew but because, as fun as working at Facebook was, there was a freedom in being somewhere else. When we arrived in Las Vegas, despite the fact that we were in the fakest city in the world, at a convention dedicated to being so far inside a computer that you can break it and everything it is linked to, for three days everything felt real.

It was Sam and Thrax's first visit, but I had fallen in love with Vegas years ago. In high school, my youth orchestra had done an exchange with the Las Vegas youth orchestra and we spent three days touring the hot Nevada desert, staring big-eyed at the towering houses of money and sex that dot the landscape. On the last day, we finally toured the famous Strip, which was less populated in the 1990s but no less grand. Perhaps it was grander then for being less dense, with casinos spaced widely apart, rising from the desert like Arabian castles. From where I sat on our orchestra's tour bus, I saw nothing against the horizon but a perfectly sun bleached, gold-accented acropolis with pillars as staunch and august as those in Rome, only brighter, bone-white against the nuclear blue sky. Our bus driver told us over the PA that Caesars Palace lacks an apostrophe because, "At Caesars, everyone is king." Taking in that man-made immensity from my shaded perch on the bus as a teenager, I had a sudden, chilling feeling that I, too, could be king.

Perhaps this is the feeling Las Vegas is designed to inspire; against the backdrop of the strip's perfect strangeness anything you could imagine seemed possible. This is its, and America's, promise. This is what makes it all okay. "This is America, you live in it, you let it happen," Thomas Pynchon wrote in a novel about the creation of a revolutionary underground mail system. "Let it unfurl."

On this second trip, at the height of the real-estate bubble, it felt like America was unfurling grandly: I was at an underground hacker convention with a gay programmer from M.I.T. and a glorified college dropout from Georgia. And we were having fun. Under the neon, away from the fishbowl of the Facebook office, where, at any time, twenty Harvard computer bros were gossiping on AIM, imagining they could track everyone's every move, we were free. Las Vegas was too big, too fake, too glittering to let anyone in it be tracked by the cool blue frame of Facebook.

"We should have stayed at the Wynn," I told Thrax and Sam when I noticed that the administrative assistant had booked them a room at the Riviera, one of the oldest casinos on the strip, with the thin, quilted, flower-print bedspreads to prove it. As soon as I mentioned the Wynn, though, I almost wished I hadn't. It would be the last time any of us ever stayed in a cheap hotel together on Facebook's dime. From what I had read of the first dot com boom six years earlier, when programmers went from working in nondescript cubicles to throwing money around on bottle service in downtown Manhattan like they were bankers in *American Psycho,* it seemed only a matter of time before we would all realize the full extent of privilege that comes with working for the next big thing on the Internet. Not just a good salary and bragging rights over your friends but the right to expect to stay in five-star hotels and sleep on 400-thread-count sheets every night.

We couldn't use our computers anywhere near the convention; the security of anything with a circuit was most probably compromised. In order to go online at all and remain in contact with Palo Alto, we had to connect via an elaborate system the boys wired in our room, draping cables over the headboard and across the floor. While the boys were at Home Depot buying cables to rig the room, I parted the faded chintz curtains to enjoy the vertiginous view of the backside of the Strip, concrete parking garages and hotel towers reminiscent of Eastern bloc buildings. I reveled in the cracked, gold-speckled Formica sink and the smoke-stained walls of our room. "Let it unfurl," felt like a goad to some grand experiment, bigger than any of us, and it was already happening.

Downstairs, the Riviera casino was at once garish and dim, thronged with pale hacker types wearing black T-shirts, shorts, and tall boots. Some had ponytails and beer guts, others were skinny punks. All were busy hacking or going to talks about hacking. The entire convention was a contest to see who could outhack the hackers, war games for people who didn't feel comfortable in sunlight. Las Vegas was the perfect host, since in the August swelter it was too hot to leave the hotel during the day.

In the elevator on our way to the conference, a *goon,* as the Defcon staffers are called, told us that the elevators had been hacked to go twice as fast as usual, and we laughed nervously as we sped the thirty floors down to the casino.

As we walked across the casino floor to a talk on hacking forms of identification (which, fittingly, I got into by wearing Sam's badge, since Sam had decided to go to the pool instead), Thrax asked passersby rhetorically, in an exaggeratedly pretentious voice reminiscent of a BBC announcer, "Are you the wheat, or are you the chaff?" The young men scurrying across the floor in their oversized T-shirts printed with the names of obscure Web sites didn't notice him, intent on winning their next hacking competition. Though the diffuse hacker community was connected twenty-four hours a day via IM and Internet Relay Chat throughout the year, Defcon is the one time where they get to come together with their people, their tribe; there are tests, levels, judgments. It felt, appropriately, a bit like being in a video game, finding our way down long hallways and bypassing the goons who guarded certain rooms.

I didn't know what Thrax considered wheat or why he was posing the question to the room, but at that moment I felt like I was the perfect actor for my role there, as girl to these boys: I knew to be graceful where the boys were gawky, savvy where they were clueless, sociable where they were awkward. I also felt, in my own way, that I was a hacker, too; I had found a side route into a technical world at Facebook where otherwise I wouldn't really belong. In computer hacking, gaining ground-floor access to a system is called *getting root,* or having the security key to the entire system, meaning you can change things or delete data at will. "If you have root, you can do anything," Dustin said sometimes as an admonition to engineers, warning them never to give up root access to Facebook to an outsider. And I was getting root.

As we were lounging on the beds in our room at the Riviera later that afternoon, avoiding the 110-degree heat outside, Thrax announced, with an air of finality, "I am going to make a reservation at the most expensive restaurant in town," as if this was a sport and finding not just any expensive restaurant but the most expensive one would score us the most points. And why not? Facebook was paying. Thrax had figured out that much about his position of privilege: that he had an expense account and that we should use it. Sam and I said nothing, continuing to stare up at the Riviera's yellowed ceiling. Though younger than us and with fewer diplomas, Thrax was the man on this trip: He was keeping the receipts, he had the company credit card, he was Facebook's green-eyed, adolescent hacker, leading man. We were just along for the ride.

Sam and I spent the afternoon at the pool at Caesars Palace, opting for the iconic hotel's opulence over the Riviera's seedy ambience. We were always looking for reasons to lie on chaises in the sun, or in the sauna in Thrax's apartment building in winter. "Oh, you guys are getting naked again," Thrax would observe matter-of-factly whenever, on social occasions, Sam and I would inevitably find the closest pool, beach, or sauna in the area and strip to our swimsuits.

Sam, unlike the rest of the engineers, adopted a wry tone in relation to all of this: the site and the company. He was a military kid whose mother was in the Air Force and acted as the family breadwinner, toting Sam and his sister around to various military bases in America and in Europe. He didn't have particular attachments to places or even to particular social milieus that the rest of us did. He knew this scene would pass and that there would be another. "You look pale," we would often say to Sam's fellow engineers in the office with affectionate sarcasm, quoting *Less Than Zero,* because it was true, and because it was funny. Everyone in the office looked pale—not because they had been away from California, like Clay in the novel, but because they lived indoors. "You look pale," Emile would sometimes say back to us, trolling, since by the end of the summer Sam and I were well-bronzed.

Thrax called us at three in the afternoon after waking up from a nap or the night before, we weren't sure. His sleeping schedule was erratic, consisting of twenty-hour days on the computer followed by sleep, from which I imagined him waking only to put his fingers back on the keypad and resume the line of code or AIM chat that he was writing when he passed out. The mere thought of this completely unregulated, unnatural sleep cycle made me imagine a sensation akin to being plugged into an electric socket at all times, minus fresh air, circadian rhythms, or exercise. His apparent lack of the need to exercise or be in nature fuelled my only mistrust of him at the time: Can he be entirely human? Most boys need to be outside sometimes, to tackle the open street, on a skateboard or a bike. I had never met anyone who could be indoors all the time, who drove everywhere, who didn't need to burn off energy outdoors. I wondered how Thrax didn't get rickets, how even his young bones could stay firm without sun.

Eventually Thrax made his way to Caesars to join us at the pool, dressed in shorts and a T-shirt that was slightly too big. Shorts on most grown-ups are automatically funny, and he must have realized that because he told us immediately that he didn't want to wear them anymore.

"I want us to go shopping to buy clothes for tonight," he declared, having made reservations at a steakhouse at The Palms, then the most expensive restaurant in Vegas (according to his extensive research). He said he could charge the new outfit to Facebook and, when I thought about it, I figured he could. A one-hundred-dollar shirt was nothing compared to $25 million or whatever our latest round of funding was (at this point, I was losing track).

Facebook was not going to buy me an outfit to wear that night, and I wasn't even going to try to slip it onto the company credit card. I'd have to wear the same American Apparel tank dress from grad school that I'd been wearing all weekend, while Thrax would don the new outfit that I would help him find. It felt ludicrous, to be shopping for VC-funded clothes for a kid who made more money than I did, but then there was nothing about the entire experience—the hacking convention, my new crew of friends, our Facebook business cards with whatever snippets of pop culture we chose to put on them, like Mark's "CEO, bitch" or Thrax's "You run, I con"—that was not, from some angle, ridiculous.

"I think we should go to Marc Jacobs," I suggested, because at the time it was my favorite store, and the idea of putting a skinny boy in a pair of skinny pants sounded like a good way to spend an hour.

"Who's that?" he asked.

I almost laughed. For all his obscure, self-taught knowledge of technology and Internet culture, he really was straight out of Georgia. "His stuff is cool, kind of mod," I explained. "You'll like it." I wasn't even sure if he knew what "mod" meant but he didn't ask.

Sam and I continued to lie on the chaises for a while, letting the glittering Vegas sun gradually slip behind the Ionic columns that circle the pool. Thrax didn't relax, leaning forward on the pool chaise, drumming his fingers against his knees. He looked at Sam and then back to me, and asked, "Is Sam coming with us?"

"Uh, yeah." I mean, I had assumed so. Sam was sitting right beside us and looked as confused as I was that this was even in question.

"I think it should be just us," Thrax said, affectlessly, flipping his hair out of his eyes with a flourish. "It's time for Sam to be the left-out one." His flinty eyes looked directly at me, as if challenging me to make a choice. What? I thought. Who is this kid? Why do we need to leave Sam out?

Despite Thrax's wish to leave Sam out and occupy the center of attention for a while, all three of us walked away from the pool and towards the Caesars Forum shops together, racing through the casino's deliberate labyrinth on a mission for what Thrax thought would be fashionable clothes. I led the boys past Agent Provocateur with a tinge of longing that told me that in my heart what I really wanted was a boyfriend who would take me to Vegas and buy me a lingerie set that I could wear because I would know he loved me, and it would be okay to be naked, vulnerable in front of him. But I, we, were not there yet. Our scrappiness was exquisite in its own way, but not yet safe, not something I could make myself completely vulnerable to. We were at a hacking convention that was about breaking things, not making them secure. Despite this, I felt better with these boys than I did with the standard, preppy engineers we had left at the office. I thought this was why I sought out the hackers rather than the Harvard bros as friends: If I had to succeed the normal way, I wouldn't make it. We had this in common.

While I felt comfortable in the hackers' company, there was also an intense opacity to them. Who were these people that the company adored, and were they people at all, or were they some kind of channel through which an American alpha masculinity was in process of remaking itself? Why else would you want a friend to be left out except to even the score in a game that you're inventing so you'll have something to win? In college and at grad school, there was a notion of politics, of some kind of larger human goal to one's work. Here, in the valley, it seemed that life was a game and the goal was just to win.

But what did it mean to win? At the time, I thought it meant that we got to be everything we imagined for ourselves, that we got to write the script to get exactly what we wanted. But what we wanted and how we would get there was not yet clear, quite.

It was a strange feeling knowing you are supposed to want to win when you aren't sure what it is you are winning.

That evening, the three of us were sitting at a table at the Palms, Thrax in a Lacoste button-down I had picked out after we spent two hours in Caesars Forum, rejecting everything else for being wrong in some way—too trendy, too fratty, too try-hard. There were celebrities in the restaurant but we barely turned our heads. We were at the center of things, even if no one else knew it yet. Thrax ordered a $175 bottle of wine that only Sam and I were old enough to drink. We poured him thimblefuls while the waiter wasn't looking, and cut zestily into our steaks, feeling more sophisticated than usual in the sleek atmosphere created by the room's mirrored columns, modern furniture, and soft lighting filtered by palm fronds. It felt, suddenly and intensely, that we had arrived.

That night, back in the hotel room, I really did have to choose between them, unlike earlier that day by the pool, since there were two lumpy Riviera beds and three of us. I didn't hesitate—it seemed right to sleep in Thrax's bed, and so I did, and the three of us talked ourselves to sleep. Thrax's hand and mine stretched near each other instinctively and I woke up later with my arm slightly touching his. His skin felt cold, almost inhuman, but I didn't pull away.

For several years, we slept this way on work trips or social ones—they were one and the same: connected, but not quite, like the physical enactment of the AIM messages we tossed back and forth just to show each other that we are here, online, si-multaneously together and apart. In retrospect it seems that this, a tangential state of connection, never total, never lost, al-ways there at midnight when you are bored or lonely and need a slight, subtle reminder that you are loved, was one of the things Facebook was about, and it was our job as employees to embody it. Thrax's and my insistence on a noncommittal proximity was the perfect manifestation of what we were creating for the whole world: a system devoted to potential connection, a way of being always near but never with the ones you love, a technology of forestalling choice in favor of the endless option, forever.

At the time, nobody, maybe not even us, quite understood this. One day, as we were driving to a pinball convention in San Jose, the song "Face to Face" by Facebook engineers' favorite band, Daft Punk, was playing on the radio: "It really didn't make sense, just to leave this unresolved." Sam blurted out in pent-up frustration, "This song is about Kate and Thrax! Why doesn't Kate just go over to Thrax's house?!" I instantly thought, but didn't say, "Because that would be too real," and I meant it—the thought of showing up at Thrax's house, looking him in the eye, and admitting that in some weird circumstantial way we liked each other seemed impossible. Because, at some point, around that time, in the little society we were constructing out of bits of code, it seemed that privacy—true intimacy—had become too scary.

CHAPTER 4

WITHIN THE MILE

*D*o you live within the mile?" employees asked often in the fall of 2006, as if testing each other's commitment to the company cause. At an All Hands meeting that April, after listing the company's latest news, such as the $25 million round of funding (at a company valuation of $525 million) that Facebook had recently received from several venture capital firms in the valley, Mark had announced, "We've decided to offer a six-hundred-dollar-a-month subsidy to employees who live within a mile of the office." The company asked engineers to be on call and able to rush to attend to site crashes or other technical crises at any moment. Engineers were issued company BlackBerrys that they kept turned on at all hours, grabbing their phones instantly upon waking to scroll through the night's engineering-related emails. Customer-support employees were hourly rather than salaried workers and thus could not legally be called on twenty-four hours a day, but we were nonetheless expected to remain alert to any critical emails and available to drop other plans and help with any last-minute testing or crisis response.

We didn't have a nonwork life: Life was work and work was life. We did this because we expected that we would be rewarded accordingly—any short-term losses, such as the option to date casually and devote energy to nonwork pastimes, would be more than compensated by long-term gain in the form of stock options we hoped would one day be worth millions of dollars. Facebook, we understood implicitly, was looking for soldiers, not journeymen. But keeping us close to our work and ready to jump into it at any time wasn't the explicit purpose of that six-hundred-dollar-per-month housing subsidy. "The reason for the subsidy is that I've heard statistics saying that people who live within a mile of their workplace are happier, and I want people to be happier," Mark explained. My immediate feeling in response to his announcement was indeed happiness, and slight surprise; he didn't usually mention mood-related words like "making people happy" at All Hands meetings, preferring to discuss technical goals like scaling and growth. But my goal for Facebook, when I thought about it, was to make people happier, and so it seemed important that we, its employees, be happy, too.

However, what we customer-support employees didn't realize when he made the announcement, was that by "people," Mark was referring to engineers, as an email that was sent out that evening to clarify the announcement explained. Engineers were the only ones covered by the subsidy, which struck all the support employees as shocking since we, with our $30,000 a year instead of their $80,000-and-up salaries, most needed it. But this privileging of technical people wasn't an anomaly. As a young designer explained to me bluntly, "Everyone upstairs is dumb," referring to the floor above the engineering lair at the 156 University office where customer support, administrators, and salespeople sat. My impulse was first to laugh at his ridiculous, blithe dismissiveness, until I realized that it wasn't very funny. The way that things were going, these guys might actually rule the world some day. And, being that I was nontechnical and, also, I believed, not dumb, I wasn't sure what this preference for engineers over anyone with a different type of skill set would mean for me.

The fact that support employees were not, in Mark's view, "people" at the company sparked a revolution. Surely, what we couldn't contribute to the company in technical skill, we contributed in social skill and compassion for users. "We thought we were all in this together," we complained among ourselves, and then in emails to executives, like Chris Kelly, Facebook's general counsel, who occupied the rare position of being both nontechnical and also somewhat important, due to his law degree and political connections to Washington. The few executives, like Chris, who understood the cost to company spirit of leaving customer-support employees out, eventually sided with us. In an announcement that Mark made just slightly apologetically at the next All Hands, the subsidy was extended to everyone. After that, almost everyone, if they hadn't already, moved within a mile of the office. It was, in retrospect, the only time employees mounted significant internal resistance to a decision Mark had made.

With everyone living nearby and our rent subsidized and food catered and even our clothes washed for free by Facebook's designated laundry service (which would also develop film, shine shoes, and mend purses if you simply dropped them off in the laundry bag every week with your clothes), we now had the makings of a self-sustaining compound from which we might never have to leave: If not a fully fledged compound, at least the perfect cast of characters and lifestyle to richly populate the pages of Facebook for our and others' entertainment. Bringing us nearer to work, in small apartments instead of gathered around a pool, was a necessary move by the company: The summer house, though only three miles away from the office, was a bit too far, a bit too fun, a bit too much of an escape from our burgeoning digital reality. There, people gathered and talked and played in real life. This next phase of the company's growth would be about making our Hotel California a virtual rather than actual reality, and this would require an absolute commitment to cause and digital country: this is where we would make the Facebook nation real.

"Are you still having fun?" Mark would ask me over the course of that year. I sometimes wondered for a second, out of curiosity, what he would say if I said *no*. He didn't speak to me much around the office except to ask this question, as if he was silently and casually monitoring the mood of nontechnical employees, wanting to check in briefly about whether we were having fun or not. I suspect he knew that if we were having fun, we would keep going, even if we weren't particularly important or well paid. So I always said *yes,* to which he always answered, "Good," and then wandered off, eyes downcast to his BlackBerry. I think he asked me if I was having fun because, on balance, I was. The whole Facebook enterprise was too strange and sudden and golden, rich with potential, not to be fascinating. How wouldn't such a wealth of ambition, boyish antics, and global potential be fun? No matter how broke and in debt I was because of my student loan, I was now indexed to an intensely wealthy venture-capital apparatus that could save us all from ever struggling with money or recognition again.

While resetting users' passwords and explaining how to resolve browser cache issues wasn't particularly exciting, odd and novel forms of Facebook usage occurred frequently that were fun to figure out. "I can't tell if this group is real or not," another customer support rep said to me from across the desk where we were all jumbled together on the third floor of the 156 University building, as the office was getting crowded with new employees. Since the previous fall, when I started, the Customer Support Team had grown from the original five people (Jake, Oliver, Maryann, Emma, and me) to over twenty employees, many of whom were Stanford humanities graduates, with graduates from a few other private colleges mixed in. He showed me a group called "If this group reaches 100,000 people my girlfriend will have a threesome." We clicked over to the profile of the group's creator and he looked real enough, with a profile photo and friends and flirtatious wall posts from girls, standard stuff for a college guy on Facebook. The group he created was growing at an absurdly fast rate, with friends seeing that another friend joined the group and joining it as well. Most of the people joining were guys.

I wondered vaguely if his girlfriend was okay with having their sex life plastered all over Facebook, but I thought it possible that she might be. American college women, after all, are known to kiss each other at parties for male attention, so this group was kind of like the virtual version of that, except that her boyfriend was the one running the show. Just another day at Facebook with another set of peculiarly Facebook problems, like discerning whether someone really wants to have a threesome, or if they are simply, in grand advertising tradition, selling sex to get publicity. It turned out, after we monitored it for a while, that this Facebook group was the first purposely designed as a viral marketing scheme—once the group had 100,000 members, its creator used it to promote a new music Web site. This scheme worked because, while what Facebook was offering users was a connection to their friends, what it offers marketers is the greatest viral distribution mechanism yet invented. In real life, you had to talk to someone to tell them you liked something: Here you could simply click a button, "join group," and Facebook would tell everyone you know.

Some college kids in the group saw that Facebook employees had joined it to monitor them, and started asking us questions on the group wall. They wanted to know what it was like to be us, employees of the site they spent all their free time on. Thrax, naturally, was glad to trumpet our riches for them: "This bacon-wrapped shrimp tastes delicious, doesn't it, Kate?" he posted on the group's wall, and then a few minutes later, "I'm going to come up to your floor for another piece of steak." The college students visibly salivated in their comments after Thrax's posts. I felt a tinge of guilt, recalling my mother saying, "You should never brag," but that sentiment seemed archaic, out of place.

The new product that we had been testing all summer and that would launch soon that fall, the News Feed, would become the most efficient way yet of distributing evidence of one's good fortune—pictures of how much fun you were having or some new thing you had bought—to all your friends. So, as we monitored the group, I could imagine the students' envy as they regarded us, these extravagant Silicon Valley clowns eating catered meats while supporting the site they used to flirt and procrastinate. In truth, the shrimp wasn't that tasty—in the early days, the caterer always overcooked and oversalted everything for the tastes of boys used to fast food—but the people watching us didn't know that. On Facebook it all sounded, and was, impossibly rich, like we were having the time of our lives and, sometimes, I think we were.

Living within the mile meant you were all-in, willing to compromise all other aspects of your life in order to remain fully available to Facebook. Some employees still chose to live in San Francisco, which gave them the option of spending time with non-Facebook employees, but that seemed like a suspect choice to those of us within the mile, whose lives revolved around the company.

While I had begun my job at Facebook with a wait-and-see, month-by-month attitude, the increasing fun and excitement encouraged me to deepen my personal investment in the company. Now that the summer house was coming to an end, I decided to go all-in and move within the mile.

I found a room in a rambling, tree-shaded house full of Stanford graduate students that felt a bit like an army barracks for academics, with thin carpet and nothing in the way of luxuries. The shower, to my unhappiness, was shared by five people. At eight hundred dollars, it wasn't cheap, but after taxes, the subsidy made it a bearable three hundred dollars per month. By this time, I was getting used to the unreal economics of Palo Alto, and my time in Baltimore had made me an expert at hacking my way through poverty: Pay rent and loan payments first, eat as cheaply as possible, preferably home-cooked meals, buy practical clothing on deep discount at Loehmann's or Neiman Marcus Last Call. There wasn't money for much else.

So, by necessity, instead of, as in Mark's case, by choice, my room was furnished with just a mattress on the floor and a laptop. It felt almost good to live a spartan existence in the midst of Palo Alto's sunny plenty, undistracted by anything but our digital mission. There was a masculine, military purity in this lifestyle that wasn't natural to me but that, like almost anything, I could play at for a while. Next to our project of connecting everyone in the world via what felt like an email system on steroids, enhanced by photographs and auto-fed updates, everything else was expendable, frivolous. And since Mark's minimalist aesthetic, expressed on his Facebook profile as a wish to "Eliminate desire for all which doesn't really matter," coincided with my financial means, I decided I would adopt a minimalist lifestyle, for lack of other options.

The role model for what it meant to be fully committed

to the mission was Dustin, who had been working tirelessly to keep the site up for over two years, never complaining, always on call, always, improbably, keeping his cool (Dustin's hard work paid off: He is now, famously, the world's youngest billionaire). I joked with him that he was the Bodie—the hard-working, street-wise young thug on *The Wire*—of the founders, hoodie up, working around the clock from his desk to secure our digital *corners,* which, in this case, meant launching new networks, monitoring traffic flow, identifying issues, fixing bugs. "Dustin a soldier," I said, echoing the voices from *The Wire,* whose accents I remembered from Baltimore. Dustin, ever modest, didn't answer, but the dark circles under his eyes some days did. As exhausted as he often looked, I admired his wholehearted dedication and thought that if they would only let me, I would be a soldier, too. I trusted Dustin, because of his dry wit and warm humility, honed no doubt by having worked at a burger stand in high school, more than Mark, whose blankness verging on haughtiness inspired only curiosity in me, so I never doubted that soldiering for the cause of Facebook, if not for Mark himself, was just.

Despite my energy and ambition to help the cause, there was no way to be a true, 'round-the-clock soldier on the customer-support team. We clocked hours on a time sheet and suffered the power trips of our recently hired head of customer support, Andreas. He was an oily, artificially tanned man who had made a career in the insincere world of corporate customer service, which made him a surprising hire, given Facebook's ideals of youthful, modern efficiency. He seemed to have been hired because the powers that be—VCs and executives—wanted a mature adult to manage customer support, rather than the twentysomethings we were (they trusted youthful nontechnical employees much less than youthful engineers). Andreas didn't understand how Facebook worked or the byzantine site rules that we were charged with enforcing, but that wasn't really his job: His job was simply to be the person assigned to be in charge of the hourly workers, like Foucault's baby in the panopticon. His power was simply in the fact that he was there, watching, even if that simply meant playing around on Facebook all day while Jake, Maryann, and I managed the Customer Support Team in practice.

Andreas hadn't attended college and seemed threatened by the fact that the team was composed mostly of newly minted Stanford grads. As customer support grew, he began pressuring us to hire the least educated people he could find. One day he asked me to interview someone who hadn't gone to college, whose resume was heavily misspelled, and whose only previous experience was working at Pizza Hut, and seemed disappointed when the person turned out to be far too unskilled in typing and writing to hire.

Customer-support employees had the least amount of power in the company, so if we wanted to escape our lowly and maligned position, we had to hack our way through and around Facebook's hierarchy one way or another. Anyone with a shred of hustle did this. There was a handsome Italian boy on our team who did next to nothing, clocking in hours he never worked, but showed up at the office just enough to smile, dark-eyed and long-lashed, at Andreas, who let his shiftlessness slide. None of us blamed the kid. It was all in the game, and in some way, everyone was playing.

The game of building kingdoms that executives from Mark down seemed to be playing reminded me of a quote from *The Wire,* "The king stay the king, unless he a smart-ass pawn." I grew more obsessed with *The Wire,* the deeper I found myself falling into Facebook's game (on weekends, I would sometimes watch an entire season and try to use it as inspiration to game Facebook's system and better my career). Someone suggested that Thrax could be Omar, the stickup artist in *The Wire* who robs drug dealers (because his MySpace hack was kind of the Internet equivalent of a stickup) but that didn't seem quite right to me. Omar had a Robin Hood politics to his piracy. He stole partly to redistribute the drug dealers' wealth to the neighborhoods they fed on. In high school, Thrax had been a pirate for piracy's sake: He had wanted to transfer media (movies, music, episodes of *I Love Lucy,* a show he openly adored) over to his servers just to have it, in the event that he might want to watch it someday and also, because having gigabytes of data at hand was part of how hackers proved their status to one another. The more media he could pirate and store on his copious hard drives, like digital stash houses, guarded by firewalls instead of guns, the better. "I'm kind of obsessed with piracy," he would say to me, later, as if even he knew this drive to accumulate data was a slightly odd, excessive pastime, a new kind of drug.

The minimalism that Mark espoused extended in my case to a minimalism of people. Without money to go out in Palo Alto (and with very little to do there if I went), I had to be selective about what I did and with whom. The Harvard guys were less careful with money, because they didn't need to be. While not typically flashy, they liked to take limos to party in the city or go wine tasting in Napa. Photo albums of these trips would always show up on Facebook afterward, full of pictures of engineers in dress shirts and ties lifting champagne glasses and rolling around on the floor of the limo, smiling with glee. I went on one Napa limo trip and, a week later, upon receiving my three-hundred-dollar share of the bill from one of the Harvard engineers, I realized that I would I have to find other ways to have fun.

So I was lucky to have Sam and Thrax as friends; their less fancy upbringings made them frugal by habit. Sam rode his bike and the bus everywhere; his apartment was furnished with a couch and the dartboard that he brought from Massachusetts in homage to the bar games of his family's working-class hometown. That fall, his sister Micaela, a clever bioscientist who dressed for the beach in short shorts and flip-flops regardless of the weather, moved from Massachusetts to live with him while she looked for work. Her social hallmark was that she proudly carried a six-pack of beer in her purse at parties, just in case the hosts hadn't supplied enough, and the Facebook engineers whose parties we went to were duly impressed and chastened: Micaela had outmanned them.

So it was that our social life in Palo Alto consisted of hanging around at our apartments playing games, like Scrabble or darts, or watching movies and, because our Facebook friends were always there, the office. When there was nothing else to do, we could always run around the empty office after midnight, tinkering with the toys and games the boys had accrued and lolling around on the body-sized bean bags that are Silicon Valley's furniture of choice. In many ways, the atmosphere of our lives that year was like an oversized preschool.

One night, after drinking on the office roof, Sam, Thrax, Justin, and another self-taught engineer, Isaac, who had been hired over a year earlier to help Mark and Dustin code until he was let go a few months later, played hide and seek happily in the dark office, amid the desks and monitors and warren-like rooms filled with blankets and video screens. During our game, I hid under the catering table obscured by the folds of a tablecloth, like Eloise at The Plaza. Thrax eventually found me because, as you do when playing hide-and-seek in childhood, I gave myself away by giggling when he came near. But, given the circumstances, how could we not laugh? We were, technically at least, adults, crawling around on the floor under computers in some of the most expensive square footage in America, waiting until our boy emperor decided it was our turn to be king. This sense that we were part of a developing royal court was bizarre, and I think accounted for the mirth everyone often felt around that time. In pictures from this period, tagged for posterity, we are almost always laughing, our faces contorted as if we can't believe our absurd good fortune. Mark never took part in these games, preferring to sit at his desk in the deep corner of the office, face illuminated by the glow of the screen. He was playing a bigger game.

Despite the financial limits of my life, I didn't feel like I was missing out. On adulthood, yes, but then, if I had been chasing the trappings of adulthood I wouldn't have been at Facebook. Adulthood meant commitments, mortgages, marriage. In the youth-fixated world of Silicon Valley, where VCs fought over the teenage boys that they wanted to hire or invest in, all of that seemed almost unimaginable, beyond reach. For one thing, the only way to afford a mortgage in the valley is to have already made your millions, and, for another, there were no men there. There were many kinds of boys, yes, but in the course of my day-to-day existence I couldn't say that anyone I interacted with, of any age, really seemed like a mature, sophisticated man. With the exception of the gray-haired Rochester, who hailed from an earlier period in the valley that seemed to be less about youthful, social glitz and more about the nuts and bolts of building software (Rochester joked about how after working at Facebook he began to wear more fashionable clothing), the oldest men there, in their thirties and forties, seemed as disinterested in anything except business victory as anyone else.

The older men in the office could be as unbridled in their wide-ranging desires for sex and attention as the younger ones. One of the few married engineers on the team was known by his female colleagues (after he had made several unwelcome propositions to them) to invite lower-ranking women at the company to have threesomes with his wife, all while trolling and starting bullying flame wars on online forums. ("Pics or it didn't happen," he retorted like any teenage Internet troll when someone sent an email to the company's social list saying that women wearing nursing bras had assembled outside the office to protest Facebook's ban on breastfeeding photos.) Like any sexual predator, he groomed people by sending them emails with innocuous, friendly banter, gradually moving in to make a sexual proposition. When I received an email from him calling me "my lady" and asking me to lunch, I quit responding to any but his most professional emails.

Within the mile, I rarely socialized with anyone who wasn't a Facebook employee. Among colleagues, we already had a scene, filled with rapt faces waiting to consume our activities and personalities both online and in the office. We also knew too much about Facebook—what features would be released and what shocking transformations of the social world would be attempted next—to let down our guard around other people, especially in the valley. It was impossible to meet anyone new at a bar or coffee shop in Palo Alto or San Francisco without the conversation turning to Facebook as soon as I mentioned where I worked. It was becoming a national obsession, and even nonemployees could, and would, talk about it for hours, as if they worked there, too. Everyone wanted to know what we were doing and what would happen next. So, given the choice between having to answer endless questions that I couldn't really answer (like what features we were going to launch or whether I could read people's messages, to which the answer was an unsayable *yes*), or staying inside our social bubble, it was easier simply not to hang out with anyone outside Facebook.

Until everyone in the world was using Facebook, anything else felt like a distraction. The unspoken goal was clear: to bring everyone on board the social network and make their lives as clean and technically efficient as our own in Palo Alto. We were so convinced that Facebook was something everyone should have that when the product team created an experimental feature called *dark profiles* in fall 2006, nobody even flinched. This product created hidden profiles for people who were not yet Facebook users but whose photographs had been tagged on the site. It reminds me now of the way members of the Mormon church convert dead people, following the logic that if they had known about Mormonism when they were alive, they would have been believers. Facebook was our religion and we believed everyone should be a member, even if they hadn't consented yet.

At the time, the fact that these profiles were called *dark* gave me slight pause. Chase, a perpetually grinning senior project manager by way of Stanford, who was in charge of keeping engineers on task, explained the project further at one of our weekly product meetings, where he explained the latest developments to the customer support team. Chase was slight in stature but carried himself something like an athletic coach, always carrying and consulting a clipboard with notes and product schedules. He had a quick, musical way of speaking that made any announcement he made sound perfectly reasonable. "You see, Mark always had this idea for a kind of Wikipedia for people, or what he called a 'dark Facebook,' where each person would have a wall and people could write anything about them on it. That was actually what he was going to make first at Harvard. But he realized that people wouldn't use something that didn't allow them to erase bad things people said about them, so he made Facebook instead." Thus, the product they had now built was a kind of compromise. People would still be added to the network whether they wanted to be or not, but at least now, should they decide to activate a Facebook account, they would have a chance to control their profiles. In a way, I had to admit that it was a bit of genius: We were using every technical means at our disposal to create a database of all the people in the world. It was the kind of information that every organization that wanted to expand its membership, including the Mormon church, would wish that they had.

While I don't think anyone came to work at Facebook precisely to have *super access,* as we called our ability to view anything and anyone on the site, regardless of the user's privacy settings, once we had that power, no one wanted to lose it. The whole product, in a sense, was a means of obtaining knowledge about other people, and as Facebook employees we had a leg up on everyone else. Another employee in engineering, a designer, was blunt about his personal motives for working at Facebook. "I built this to find you," said a quote he inserted as an *Easter egg* (a programming term for an intentional hidden message in a Web site or video game) on the search page. The designer's words perfectly captured the intent that drives much of people's Internet usage: to search for partners, whether sexual or romantic, in the easiest and quickest way possible.

Social network usage statistics indicate that men and women have different online viewing habits: Two-thirds of the photos viewed on social networks, Harvard researcher Mikolaj Piskorski found, are of women. "Men prefer looking at women they don't know, followed by looking at women they do know. And women prefer looking at other women they know." Consumption of men's photos is proportionally the smallest segment of viewing behavior, suggesting that women are less interested in consuming men's photos than heterosexual men are interested in viewing photos of women they've never met. In the end, no matter how much we tried, we couldn't use technology to produce love. Because love, unlike technology and its uses, requires commitment to one, instead of the broadcast and consumption of many bits of distant, digital content. Love doesn't scale.

At the time, however, the knowledge and the power and the wealth we were developing would be too intoxicating for us to care about something as unquantifiable as an intimate feeling. We were all, I think, lonely on some level, but the answer wasn't to find love and another life away from Facebook: The answer was to work harder, scale faster, and get bigger, and love would be waiting for us somewhere at the end. Everyone wanted to be king, first, myself included. The rest could follow.

On September 5, 2006, after we had been testing it all summer, Facebook finally released its first and perhaps, to date, most controversial new product: News Feed. Before News Feed, Facebook had been a comparatively discreet book of profiles, maintained and updated individually by each profile owner. News Feed introduced a new homepage where any and all updates to a friend's profile might appear as a broadcast story, with a headline and accompanying photographs. Your friends' activities on Facebook were now news, and your homepage was a kind of social newspaper.

However controversial, the News Feed was new, and whatever is new or new-seeming (because most so-called innovations in Silicon Valley are combinations of other products and ideas) must be built, launched, and used by as many people as can be convinced to use it. So, News Feed was launched to all users, in one fell swoop. I stayed up until midnight the night before the launch, lying on my bed in my bare room, to watch as the product was pushed out. Back then, we always pushed at midnight, since that was when traffic was lowest and all engineers were awake. One minute the homepage was blank, boring, harmless, safe. The next minute it was full of stories, of what someone was doing now, of a new friendship made, of a relationship ended. The automated literature of our lives had begun.

If my early response to the product that summer was one of unease, users reacted with an entirely different magnitude of distress. The day we launched News Feed felt, without exaggeration, like a minor Vietnam, complete with helicopters and reporters circling the office to videotape the protesters who threatened to appear in our courtyard. I arrived at the office feeling jittery and gun-shy, having lain awake all night wondering what the reaction would be when college students on the East Coast woke up to find that their lives had been serialized overnight.

Email after email of the thousands we received that day told graphically of the betrayal and evisceration the users felt. Phrases like "I feel violated," and "You've ruined my life" were common, and the emails were long and passionate, filled with all the personal details and drama that they felt Facebook had exposed without warning. "I just broke up with my girlfriend yesterday and thanks to your 'News Feed' everyone on campus saw a story about it this morning! How would you like it if people started publishing stories about your life without telling you?" one user howled.

I did nothing all day but sit at my desk reading the agonized emails and responding to them with a stock, impassive answer along these lines: "This information was already available to your friends on Facebook; we're just delivering it more efficiently." Sometimes, I modified the stock response with an acknowledgment of the user's story and feelings, just to sound a bit more human, like I cared, which I did, because at some basic, human level, I sympathized with their feelings. If I hadn't known the News Feed was coming, I would have been shocked and upset, too.

As the day progressed and the email continued to flood in, I started to feel brutalized myself: The pain, anger, confusion, and shock expressed by the users was real, even if the product itself meant no harm. By midnight, there were still thousands of emails in the queue, and it became clear that we were never going to get through them all. As always, there was a technical solution: With the click of a button, Jake blasted the stock News Feed response email to everyone who had written in that day, whether their query had to do with News Feed or not. I left the office and wandered home down Palo Alto's empty Hamilton Street, bleary-eyed and emotionally battered, looking forward to losing consciousness in sleep.

I suppose that the users' shock at News Feed stemmed, in addition to the feeling of being suddenly exposed, from a sense that, overnight, without warning, their online presences had gone from static profiles to live-updating digital characters, put in narrative form for others' enjoyment. Were they ready to be characters dancing perpetually in the virtual courtyard of Facebook's Hotel California for our friends' entertainment? Whether or not they were ready, it had happened.

This was always the case with social-media technology: It meant no harm, but that did not mean that it would not cause it. This is how technology is pure, and this is why people love it so much. Ascribing intentionality or an emotional impact to a piece of technology or what it does is impossible, and the product that is built mediates between the intentions of its creators and its users. Technology is the perfect alibi. Facebook doesn't hurt people: People hurt people. This is true. But just as Facebook makes it possible to do things faster, more efficiently, more cheaply, it makes it possible to hurt people faster, more efficiently, with less cost to themselves. It removes any sense of direct responsibility for our behavior, for how what we do makes others feel. With Facebook, you can act and be seen acting without ever having to look anyone who is watching you in the eye, or look at them at all.

In a tense All Hands meeting a day after the News Feed launch, Mark, responding to employee fears that we had badly alienated users to the point of fleeing the site, predicted that the controversy would settle. Four days later, it became clear that he was right. To mollify users and perhaps also anxious employees, executives, and VCs, Mark consented to the addition of privacy controls that allowed users control over what profile updates could appear in a News Feed story.

But, in this, as in future cases, the users got over it. They had to; they had no choice, and we knew it. The only competitor of Facebook in 2006 was MySpace, and MySpace didn't even count, with its hard-to-read, glittery fonts, wildly decorated pages, and absence of technical advancement. When people asked us, "How are you going to beat MySpace?" we acted as if we didn't even hear the question, looking off into the distance in the manner of Mark, who was asked to answer this question often by press and investors. "They are doing something different," he would say, and, by that, it sounded like he meant, "They don't even matter to us." MySpace's focus on individual self-expression in a clunky, technically primitive interface was not where the Internet was going, in Mark's parlance. The Internet was heading in the direction of replicating not just individual identities but the relationships between individuals—or maybe, ambitiously, the entire social world as such—and Facebook was already doing that better and more comprehensively than any other service.

As if they knew that employees desperately needed a release after our week of doing battle in the social-media trenches, the company obtained tickets for all of us to go to a Dave Matthews concert. I didn't even like Dave Matthews that much, but it was with relief that I left the office early that Friday to dress for the concert and put accusations of technological "rape" and "betrayal" out of my mind. I picked out one of my old college-style outfits, as if willing myself back on campus studying literature, instead of serving as an accidental private in a social-networking war.

In keeping with the camp-cum-college atmosphere of the company, our party planners always arranged for buses to transport us directly from the office to company parties and back. In a small gesture of resistance, Sam and I would always go to the dive bar across the street (it was divey by Palo Alto standards, at least, with plain décor, lower prices, and an Erotic Photo Hunt machine that we played often on breaks from work) for a grown-up Manhattan, dark with whiskey and bitters, before boarding the bus like so many teenagers headed to prom night. Like everything anyone at the company did, our archaic preference for whiskey over vodka would be immortalized in a Facebook group, called the "Society for Anachronistic Alcohol," which was created by Harry, a saxophone-playing engineer whom Rochester brought in from his former company. The group name itself became anachronistic, because in two years everyone would be drinking whiskey, thanks to *Mad Men* and the emergent pop culture of vintage masculinity.

Facebook had rented a VIP area for us at Shoreline Amphitheater, Silicon Valley's concert venue, which sits in a stale-smelling bog across from Google headquarters. This was the first such designation for most of us, and it felt exciting. VIP-ness was something that someone else, more important and with more money, always had, but now we were skipping the lines and walking directly to our own private area, where we could observe regular concertgoers from behind a fence and, in turn, be observed. The whole point of VIP treatment, it seems, is to speak to our universal human desire to feel special, valuable, desired: And to have something that others don't. When we were VIPs, as Thrax might have put it, it is time for everyone else to be the left-out ones.

In the VIP section, we milled about, talking to each other while drinking wine or beer from the open bar and, mostly, feeling relieved that we were no longer in the throes of the News Feed tumult. It had only been days since the feature launched, but days in Internet time are like weeks in regular time: Even twenty-four hours is enough to put distance between you and an Internet phenomenon. Harry seemed already to have intuited this—that anything that happens online will pass—as he looked placid at the party, just as he had all week while employees were biting their fingernails and attempting to remain calm. Or, perhaps, he simply didn't care how users felt about News Feed as much as I and some other employees, judging from the strained, worried looks on their faces all week, did.

Regardless of our feelings about the new technology we had just unleashed on the world, the traumatic events of the week brought us closer to each other, as a battalion must feel after a skirmish, and we huddled in circles chatting, feeling united against our users mobbing us from across the Internet.

As the sun set on the lawn, we moved to our seats close to the stage. Our VIP treatment enhanced the de facto sense of entitlement that we, as Facebook employees, were beginning to feel. We felt entitled because we had just built a device—News Feed—that replaced the organic word of mouth and socially networked communities that made bands like Dave Matthews popular. A band's fame spreads when people discover them and start telling friends, but News Feed now made it possible for people to spread their taste in music instantly by listing favorite bands on their profiles. We knew that there would be much power in this. The only thing more powerful than celebrity is to own the tool that makes it.

However, the Dave Matthews band was of a previous, pre-digitized time: all guitars and instruments, instead of the electronic music that looped constantly in the office. The music was real, and the night felt more palpable and present than anything else since those days in August when we had escaped the virtual unreality of Palo Alto for the authentic unreality of Las Vegas. My heart sang a little at the music, at the way everything felt, at the flick of Thrax's pale hair on my nose as he talked into my ear. It was nice to feel things, rather than watch text and images scroll by. At one point I looked behind us and saw that Rochester, old-time computer geek and valley billionaire twice over, was dancing.

On the bus back to the office, Thrax and I sat curled up companionably, holding hands, watching the dark Peninsula sky pass by outside the window, but we stopped short of a kiss. "I can't have a relationship story show up in News Feed," he explained, and I filed that away in my groggy, battle-scarred head as a perfect statement to summarize what had happened that week. The narratives Facebook wanted to tell about us already had the upper hand, and News Feed had only launched three days ago.

As the winter came and the engineers were consumed by work, racing to build the next wave of features, I retreated into my own hobbies—writing, painting, taking long walks to Stanford's Lake Lagunita and back—almost forgetting about technology for a while. I left my computer at the office when I went home, and since the company didn't give customer-support staff BlackBerrys, at the time the smart phone of choice, I still had an old Samsung flip phone that delivered nothing in the way of data. When I was away from the office, I was effectively off the grid, though I was still in the heart of it.

I watched our lives overlap with technology at an ever-increasing pace, as News Feed quickly grew central to people's sense of their social worlds and smartphones became everyone's favorite toy, and grew almost nostalgic for the rough edges and unprogrammed contrasts of Baltimore. The whole city of Baltimore is a patchwork of rich and poor, green and gray, black and white, and I missed it. I worried that I was getting soft in the medium sheltered tones of Palo Alto, where no one seemed aware of how dark or how light and beautiful the outside world can be. In Baltimore, the view of all of it—and the corresponding awareness that the world was full of people with different circumstances and experiences, particularly ones less fortunate than your own—was inescapable. In Palo Alto, there were houses, shops, a few offices, and many computers all talking to one another, each pretty much the same as the other. But I knew that the rest of the world was full of people poorer, darker, and less technologically provided for than the engineers were in Palo Alto, and this lack of awareness on their part was draining. Here, it was like we were living in a fantasy of perfect wealth, where everyone was the same and everyone was equal, but *everyone* was defined as young engineers competing for the same crown.

CHAPTER 5

VIDEO NATION

*B*y Facebook's third birthday in February 2007, the site had 15 million users and the company had at least 150 employees. We had bypassed the famous Dunbar's number that Mark cited often as an archaic, real-world social limit that Facebook had to succeed in making obsolete. Anthropologist Robin Dunbar proposed in a 1992 article that approximately 150 is the maximum number of people that any individual was able to know and keep up with at a given time. So, as the company sailed past 150 employees, our internal society would be a test of how well Facebook can help us manage social contacts and, in Mark's words, stay connected, despite our growing number.

On this February afternoon, the sun flooded the third floor of the office, where administrative assistants were rushing hurriedly to prepare for the party. By three o'clock, the room was festooned with blue balloons, blue cakes, and kegs. Employees in navy-blue hoodies that said *Facebook* across the front—the first of our many unofficial company uniforms, which change whenever the designers concoct a new riff on the Facebook logo, were drinking and playing Beirut on tables set up for the occasion. As at all our parties, professional photographers roamed the room taking pictures of employees practicing their most flattering poses—hand on hip, smile wide, like we were the happiest people in the world. And, at parties like this, we were happy, because we got to do what Facebook did best: enacting and documenting a uniform, unspecific glee, a moment with no larger concerns, in which everyone smiles on command, with nothing to fear from the ever-present cameras and their incessant need to document us.

I had a specific reason for my happiness, beyond Facebook's birthday and the almost parental relief I felt that the enterprise we had all been working tirelessly on was entering its third year. Whatever this toddler network was, and intended to be, it was going to be huge, I was sure. I was also ecstatic because in four hours I would be taking my first long vacation since I began working at Facebook. I would be boarding a flight to Rio de Janeiro, back to Ipanema and its glorious beaches, and away from all of the digitally prompted smiling and poking and constant virtual coddling. For the past four Spartan months of work, I was completely dedicated to Facebook's cause, but also saving every penny in order to spend three weeks away. At some atavistic level, I missed a world where everything wasn't planned for me, where things weren't always new and gray and clean, where I was forced to be present in the flesh, confronted with situations I couldn't preview and manage remotely.

I bought the cheapest ticket to Brazil I could find, a five-hundred-thirty-dollar round-trip ticket on Taca Airlines, on a Southwest-sized 737 that was too small to make the full journey to the southern hemisphere and had to stop in Panama to refuel. As we winged out of SFO and onward toward the tropics that night, the flight became turbulent and children on the plane screamed in Portuguese for hours. I remembered the story Micaela told one night at a Palo Alto bar about when she and Sam were children and flew between Army bases on planes with nothing but seatbelts tethering them to the floor, and that they cheered whenever there was an exciting patch of turbulence and wished for more. While I wasn't afraid of flying to Brazil by myself, I wasn't fearless enough to cheer on this roller-coaster ride far above the Amazon. It's funny how we choose what we are going to be afraid of. I can wander the streets of any city alone, but quiver at the thought of jumping blithely off rainforest waterfalls like the Hopkins surfer boys did on my previous trip to Brazil. It made me think of the computer hackers, who fear nothing when it comes to waging war on other people's virtual property, but cringe at the idea of exploring unfamiliar urban climes.

"Why aren't you going to Brazil with Kate?" Sam asked Thrax, vaguely accusingly, over IM, as I watched. Sam, Thrax, Justin, and Emile were all freaked out that I was going to Brazil alone, without friends or Facebook people (which was basically the same thing), but didn't want to betray they cared by actually saying so. "I don't have the balls," Thrax answered ruefully. I could see him picturing kidnappings and beheadings, as if all of Rio de Janeiro were like the deadly, warring *City of God*. Just the thought of a suburban American hacker suddenly immersed in

Rio's cacophonies of carnival music and street dancing seemed almost impossible, as if the sensory overload would instantly overwhelm the circuitry of someone used to sitting alone in the dark, behind a screen. I realized this was why I was going back to Brazil, because despite the fact that I had found friendship and fun at Facebook, there was another side of me—one that loved discussing romance languages rather than programming them—that felt neglected and in need of sun. If no one from work wanted to go with me, it was fine. It was time for me to go on an adventure of my own, and for them to be the left-out ones.

Landing in Rio de Janeiro after the long flight over the tropics was almost more of a relief than it was two years earlier. At the time, I was running from the ascetic world of academia; now I was running from an intense focus on administering a growing digital world. Comfortingly, Rio de Janeiro was unchanged, awash in golden light and lightly dressed bodies and the constant sound of samba. After checking in at the fifteen-dollar-per-night hostel on Rio's hostel row, I ran directly to my beloved Ipanema beach, where the sands were alive with light and the play of bodies. People tossed soccer balls back and forth and played in the surf as hawkers called out, "Agua de coco, cerveja," almost as though they were singing. There was too much to look at to focus on anything in particular, so I just took in the colors and the way it all felt: soft sand, the green of palms, the whitest light. Without a second thought, I lost track of time and the accumulated anxiety of living in a world where I was expected to be focused on a screen and be virtually available all the time.

I hung out on the beach during the day and ventured out

into the samba clubs at night with new friends made on the stoop of the hostel, all visiting from somewhere, all going somewhere else next. It made me realize that, socially, the *now* of travelling, which consists of whoever is there, in whatever place you've all happened to end up at the same time, is more natural for me to inhabit than the *now* of the Internet, a disembodied world which includes everyone, everywhere, all somewhere else, behind some other screen.

Some nights later, I was in the southern Brazilian beach town of Florianopolis, and my local hostel crew ventured to an outdoor reggae bar on a sea of sand dunes. While waiting for the band to start, a few of us walked far up into the dunes until we could see nothing but sand and sky in every direction. Someone tried to take a picture, but the moonlike stillness couldn't be captured; the light was too diffuse to make sense to the camera. I thought of my colleagues back in California and how they would be awed by this dark sublimity in the midst of a strange and wild continent, so raw and far from anything they had experienced. I wanted them to see it, or better experience it, since the moment was so much bigger than the view: It was the velvet vastness, the utter quiet, the slight wind brushing sand against our skin, the far-off glow of the bar we'd left behind. I left the dunes feeling certain that life was still meant to be lived, not continuously filmed, mediated, and watched from afar.

On my return to Palo Alto three weeks later, I rediscovered that, in the new world we were building, living life without technological mediation would be a luxury. At work, we usually approached each other with a swift efficiency, anxious to rush off to some online business, but now I lingered and smiled when I ran into coworkers in the hallway, still basking in the memories of my vacation. When in conversation at happy hour with Chris Kelly, Facebook's general counsel, whom I regaled with stories of my Brazilian adventures, I saw his face register a surprise and slight confusion that my Brazil-influenced personality was different, my presence calmer and more open to conversation. I had a brief panic that perhaps I should mask my joy at being present instead of a mere vessel from which controlled Facebook posts and comments flowed. Within a week, though, my behavior readjusted to the Palo Alto norm and my Brazilian warmth was gone: I conducted myself blank-faced, keeping conversations at work to a cold minimum, saving the information transmission for email, IM, and Facebook. I was back.

Still, having been away from it, I was more unnerved now by the office's intense devotion to the screen, so I lay low, finding a shallow substitute for the Brazilian sea by moving to a new apartment building with a pool, still within the mile. I could barely afford it but I felt, after Brazil, that a pool was necessary, as though it could fix things, if only because the splashing water wasn't safe for technology. The apartment was in a 1920s Mission-style building called the *Casa Real* whose Craigslist listing promised that it was once the home of the rich and famous of Palo Alto, though at the time it was a poorly maintained, overpriced money factory like all the other apartment complexes in town. The fact that I lived at the *Casa Real* is an irony that is not lost on me. *Real* in this case meant "royal," but in the heart of the city that aims to digitize our lives, I interpreted it differently.

That spring, I noticed that one of the designers, Ariston, a soccer-playing Duke graduate who was fanatical about movies and talked about wanting to make feature films one day after his Facebook millions were secured, was frequently updating his status on Facebook with the word *motion*. He was telling us all something, virtually, loudly, but in code. *Motion,* I found out late one night at the office while talking to Emile and Thrax, was the code name for what would be known as *Video,* a project that Ariston and Thrax were developing on their own, without Mark's direction or consent. Typically, in order for a Facebook feature to be developed, it had to be part of the product road-map, which was a six-months-out plan that was overseen and approved by Mark and that determined what products would be built and when and who would work on them. In this case, Thrax and Ariston didn't care to wait for the roadmap to catch up to them: They wanted Video, and they wanted it as soon as possible, so late at night they sneaked into the screen- and blanket-laden room off the engineering floor and built Video.

Years later, the building of Video would be described in a Facebook recruiting advertisement as a "brilliant hack" that proved how maverick and self-directed the engineers were. But, in truth, making Facebook Video was not a radical disruption so much as it was, like most of Silicon Valley's products, an evolution and combination of various existing products, an obvious next step for the company's suite of technologies. After all, video already existed on YouTube, which was founded by a former Facebook employee who had left a month before I started, and on the streaming video site that Thrax had already built in college. The fact that Facebook later used the story of Video's maverick origins as a recruiting tool shows how the making of Video was a culturally vital act of rebellion for Facebook; you can't claim the identity of a hacker company if your engineers aren't breaking any rules.

So, while Thrax and Ariston did not invent video, they were compelled to bring it to the company and claim it as Facebook's own (like all of Facebook's products, such as Photos, the product was simply and grandly called Video, as if it were the one and only). Their compulsion wasn't just to disobey orders and build something they weren't supposed to, but, in the spirit of the company, to strive toward a monopoly. The would-be kings did not come to Facebook to only half digitize the world, to own a record of text and still images. They wanted to own moving images. They wanted to see everything. They wanted to film everything. They wanted no limitation on the documentation and distribution of our lives, or the degree to which they could access the lives of others. And finally, perhaps, they wanted to be stars, by building the technology so that they could make the movies that would make them and everyone around them stars. As if to drive this home, the Facebook Video frame was fashioned in the form of a movie screen: wide and black, as though we were watching ourselves in a theater. If there was anything prescient about this in 2007, it was that the world wasn't yet in a place where everyone wanted to use technology to make them a star.

In fact, the idea that building this technology could make you visible to the world like a celebrity, or even turn you into a celebrity, didn't really occur to me then. In 2007, Facebook still seemed as though it was gaining value precisely by being private, by showing you what you would have seen anyway offline: the intimate lives of people you were already intimate with, private moments that you had participated in. Mass fame seemed like the confused pursuit of actors in another medium: reality television. At the time, the only people I was connected to on Facebook were people that I knew and with whom I shared real-life social experiences. I couldn't fathom yet why you would want everyone, even people you've never really known, to know you.

To me, Facebook Video was just another gadget to play with, but a little gratuitous at that point, technology for technology's sake. The test videos Thrax uploaded overnight as he built the product seemed to make this point over and over: They were scenes from an empty, dark office, scenes of faces flickering at the camera, saying nothing, fiddling with their floppy hair. Nothing happened in them and I wondered what impulse caused him to click record. Why this moment and not the one five minutes later? I always wondered that when I saw that a new video had been posted.

The lack of action or purpose in the test videos perfectly represented the motivation behind these projects: to technologize everything, just to say that we did. The televising and digitization of private life was the new colonialism: without any continents left to explore and own, private life had become the last frontier. "Television Rules the Nation," a hidden quote that Thrax and Ariston inserted in the header of the Facebook Video page, was visible only to those who knew to highlight it with their cursors. When everyone would be using Facebook, the technologists would have captured life itself, all the moments in our lives that used to be belong only to the people who lived them. To own not the physical map of the world but the map of human life was, I began to think, the goal.

As a woman and a customer support employee I was expected, for the most part, to follow the engineers' leads, because we were a technical company and this implied that what we were doing required technical skills. The trouble was that I also embodied Facebook's ethos of rebellion all too well, and there was no role available, at the time, for a woman who broke the rules. I did my job and accomplished my goals, but beyond that I didn't feel compelled to fall in line. I knew that if I simply did everything I was told, I would not be of any interest to Mark, who preferred employees who were slightly dangerous, like the cyberpunk characters in the 1990s movie *Hackers* that he and many other engineers referenced often. I decided I would develop my own project, off the grid, and in a nontechnical capacity.

While Thrax was building Motion/Video, Sam and I stayed up late some nights to prepare and launch Facebook networks in other countries. First, I would have to gather all the metadata about university networks abroad (like the names of schools, their locations, and their web domains, which we would use to authenticate students as legitimate members of their school's Facebook network). Then, Sam would run a script he had written that would build the networks and check for any issues before declaring them live and ready for registrations. Once the networks had been launched on a given night, usually around midnight or one o'clock in the morning, we would toast to our new territories. On the Watch Page, a page Dustin developed that allowed us to see how many Facebook users were registered in any given Facebook network, we would observe as users instantly began signing up for the new networks we had created. Next to the name of each network, a count depicting its number of users would steadily mount upward, first in the single digits, then growing into the hundreds. If we were doing really well, it could reach into the thousands overnight.

Building new networks abroad was fun and independently motivated, a very Facebook thing to do in the company's developing corporate mythos of the self-starting employee, and good for the site's growth. As such, our work was to be rewarded. However, as in any corporate hierarchy, any time people went around the rules at Facebook, it unsettled middle management. "You are doing an excellent job in customer support, but I've noticed that you are working outside the department," Andreas told me in a performance review that spring, his eyes narrowing, wanting me to be afraid. He was more concerned with maintaining company hierarchy than, as the rest of us were, getting critical work done by any means necessary. It's possible he didn't stop to think that the networks abroad needed to be launched in order to build momentum for Facebook's growth outside the United States. While Andreas didn't understand this, Dustin did: One night, when I was hanging out with Sam at his desk on the engineering floor, Dustin tacitly encouraged us to launch more networks. "He's your boy," Dustin said to me, gesturing to Sam. He knew that the company had lucked out with us: We were doing work without his even having to ask. This, like Thrax making Video, was the startup dream: that the product you are making is so compelling that your employees will advance it in their sleep, or at least in the time when they should be sleeping.

So, I nodded and pretended to listen while my manager chastised me, and then, late at night, continued to launch new networks with Sam anyway. This dissonance between upper and middle management is what happens when you work for a company like Facebook, which is simultaneously about control and the dismantling of control. Facebook wanted to disrupt the market without having its own order disrupted, to perpetually change and break things without allowing its users the same privilege. Internally, it was the same: Engineers were tacitly encouraged to break rules while the rest of the company had to follow them, unless they had some tricks of their own. The people in the company who could get around this paradox were the ones who could *social* it (the short term for *social engineering,* or hacking one's way around something using social means) by breaking the right rules and, above all, remaining popular, and in doing so riding all the inherent corporate contradictions as far as they would take them. Facebook's work environment, like much of Silicon Valley, and even like the Internet itself, was always about power: about maximizing your own power while conceding as little of it to others as you could.

Maybe as reward for my labor or maybe because he just happened to have an extra ticket, in April 2007 Dustin bestowed a ticket to the Coachella music festival on me. All of my friends at the company were going, but at three hundred dollars per ticket plus three days of lodging expenses, sadly, I didn't have the money to go. So, when Dustin gave me the ticket I felt like Cinderella with the glass slipper: I could go to the ball in the desert. I hadn't left Palo Alto since my trip to Brazil two months earlier and I was, as always, anxious to leave—light and heat and live music were as essential to me as coding and Python (the preferred programming language in the valley) were to my coworkers.

As the sun was going down over Palo Alto, Justin, Emile, and Thrax picked me up in Justin's Honda (later, everyone drove Audis, but no one had that kind of money yet, so mostly we drove practical Japanese sedans) at my apartment for the long drive to Coachella. We always did everything at night, since everything in the valley was cooler and more vital in the dark, and driving was no exception. We would be in the car for six hours, traveling past garlic-scented Gilroy and onward to the flat dreariness of the I-5 and, finally, outward to Palm Springs. I assumed that we would sit and talk and listen to music like my friends and I always did on the drives to Los Angeles from Phoenix, but this was a different time and a different kind of road trip. As we drove into the darkness of the I-5, computers and gadgets started to come out of custom-made Facebook messenger bags and were turned on.

While I was resting against the headrest in the backseat, trying to sleep, I saw the telltale glow through my eyelids of the laptop screen bobbing in front of me. "Noooo, not again, not here," I thought. I understood the constant presence of photos and video at parties but in the car? While I was sleeping? "Kate's going to hate me forever," Thrax said to the screen, turning it on

me, "Talk." The video camera on his MacBook Pro was record-
ing my nap, which was now over. It was my job to perform. So,
I talked about nothing into the camera, addressing Jamie, who
was sitting at home watching us on Facebook from his sandbox.
Sandboxes were testing areas that occupied what was called the
developer tier of the site, which only engineers and other employees could access. Engineers would play in their sandbox as they
developed new code for the site, and only when the code was
fully developed would they migrate the code to the live site at
one of the weekly midnight pushes. While I talked to the camera, Thrax narrated the scenery passing by. "Buses welcome," and
"Daylight headlight section," he read off the highway signs. "I
think we're in the middle of nowhere." We were indeed in the
middle of nowhere, but I kept talking to our distant audience,
and Emile did too. Then we signed off, "We love you, Jamie,"
we said, and at that moment it sounded like we did, although
it wasn't something we'd say to him in person. I think we could
tell him we love him because he was so far away, and to love him
is to love the technology that allows us to speak to him anyway,
safely, intimately, from afar. Our technology, ourselves: For us, at
the heart of this revolution, they were ever increasingly the same.

From the minute Thrax's project began to be built, forcing
each other to perform in videos became a kind of a company
ritual: Video was most often used by Facebook employees for
practical jokes. At a party, someone would turn a camera on
and pretend to be setting up for a photo, but after everyone was
posed and moue-ing, they would reveal that it was a video all
along. The subjects of the video would shriek when they realized
what had happened, everyone would collapse into laughter, and

the video would always be posted to Facebook for everyone to watch and laugh at. The joke never seemed to get old.

After we all finished speaking dutifully into the camera, Thrax posted the video to his sandbox in the development tier for other Facebook employees to view. Employees often loaded Facebook from this tier because it gave us access to new things that weren't available on the site yet (one caveat about using a development version of Facebook was that things were often broken and buggy there, so one never knew whether a wall post would go through or a photo would appear). Other employees, who were sitting at their desks in Palo Alto, posted comments on Thrax's video to say they saw me sleeping in the video five minutes before. This is bizarre, I thought. We are still in the car, locked in a glass bubble in the middle of Joan Didion's beloved Central Valley with farm-land on either side, and already people have been able to watch our carbound activities. Why is this kind of immediate sharing of our most mundane moments with distant friends even a thing that is happening? The answer to this question, as with all the things that Facebook made over the years, was that the sharing was happening because it could. If it could be built, it must be, and we must be, if not the first, then the biggest builders of this and every other thing. This was the code of the valley.

Thrax and Emile entertained themselves by filming more videos and sending them back to Facebook, and reading the comments on the videos that were posted immediately by our colleagues in Palo Alto. It was a perfect, near-live feedback loop: We couldn't be alone for a second, even in a moving car. And, apparently, our activities in the car were more interesting than whatever the people back home were doing, because they couldn't resist watching and commenting on them. It is an odd logic, this, but it is the logic the social net depends on: That because something or someone you know was filmed, it becomes interesting, worthy of watching. Technology and distance make us more fascinating to each other.

Midway to Palm Springs, we stopped at a truck stop to buy drinks and stretch. There was a store next to the convenience mart full of fake guns and firecrackers, and Emile, Thrax, and Justin bought them, playing cowboys in the parking lot at three in the morning. This made more sense to me as a thing to do with friends on a highway in the middle of the night. Of course, Thrax was making a video of this activity that he would post to the site as quickly as was technically possible. However, because we were in Bakersfield in the center of absolutely nowhere, his Sprint data card didn't work and we had to return to a strictly analog existence for the last hours of the drive. The boys' fingers itched with nervousness, drumming loudly against their knees in the dark, unmediated hush of the car. When technology failed, they had nothing to do.

It was too early to show up at the house we had rented, so we stopped at the Cabazon outlet mall on an Indian reservation, where every retail brand has an outlet and where the winds from the desert sweep unrelentingly across the asphalt, like a Sahara in a strip mall. I felt better when we were shopping because, unlike hacking, it was familiar territory. This was the one activity where my companions would consent to follow my lead. "I think you should wear linen shorts," I told them, since we were going to the Empire Polo Field, where Coachella is held.

The name Empire Polo Field struck me as appropriate for

us because, in a way, we were like colonists, but for the social Internet instead of land. When other people saw the crowds at Coachella, they saw faces; we saw profiles on new Facebook accounts. We knew they would all have a Facebook profile one day.

At the mall, we went to Ralph Lauren and searched the aisles full of fake palm trees and golf shirts for linen, which they, of course, had. As we were leaving, one of Thrax's friends called from Georgia, and we stood around in the windy parking lot while they talked in Southern accents so strong I could hear a drawl oozing through the phone. I leaned closer to absorb the accent: It was so thick and real, from a place I could barely imagine. His friend wanted to come to Coachella but couldn't afford it, and I was reminded how lucky I was that Dustin gave me his ticket.

We left the mall for the vacation house, where Chase and his crew of Stanford graduates were already ensconced. I made Brazilian caipirinhas out of copious limes and lemons for everyone, and pretended in all the stark sunshine that I was in Brazil again, even though I was surrounded by my pale coworkers of Silicon Valley. Thrax wandered around with his video camera, as always taping everything and nothing: the kitchen countertop strewn with booze and bags of chips, the pool, the people lying on chaises. They waved idly at the camera when it was pointed at them, saying *hello*. "You shouldn't film for so long as you are walking into the room," Chase said, "It makes the video look like a porno." I suppose that Chase was right in a way: The taping of everything made it feel like we were in a porn movie, without the sex, but with all the weird, awkward exposure of our private presences to an audience we couldn't see. Thrax agreed, but nothing changed. The camera was always on.

Each morning at Coachella we parked the car in the dusty lot of the Polo Field and walked across acres of horse-soiled dirt to get to the entrance. (Years later, everyone would be rich enough to buy VIP passes and bypass the dusty march, but for now this was a long, dreaded, communal part of the Coachella ritual.) We made lazy commentary on the long walk in for the camera, MTV VJ style, about the fashions of Coachella: As usual, there were moccasin boots and American Apparel shorts that year, as if everyone were living a three-day Western desert fantasy, like *Casablanca* for Palm Desert. I was reminded of my favorite writing professor's injunction that we "Make up movies for ourselves to star in; write the lines." Life was exactly like that, everything was a line and a scene, except that these movies were really being filmed, and we had to invent our characters on the spot.

Once we got through security we raced to see Ratatat, whose metallic chords and looping beats were, along with Facebook's musical heroes, Daft Punk, one of the soundtracks of 2007, introspective and masculine and hazy, like a long desert drive or a programmer's long code session. After the set we stood around on the lawn, forming a small island in a sea of people all racing to find something to see. The cell towers on the polo field were overloaded by phones grasping for signals, and we lost all the bars of connectivity on our devices. Rendered inconsolable by the loss of connection, Justin stared at the screen of his Black-Berry, changing position every few minutes to see if he could find a signal. His new BlackBerry Pearl had just been released that week and, even though it was signalless, as we stood on the grass illuminated by the setting sun, he proclaimed it beautiful, touching its curved lines with love. It was as if this new smart phone carried all the secrets of the world, like the conch shell in *Lord of the Flies.*

Back at the house that night, we collapsed on the living room floor in exhaustion, too tired to continue the party into the early hours of the morning, as many Coachella concertgoers do. There weren't enough bedrooms for all of us, and Chase's group had done the work of renting the house, so they got the rooms and Emile, Thrax, Justin, and I slept on blankets on the floor. As we were nodding off to sleep at around two in the morning, Sean Parker, the Napster co-founder and early Facebook employee, who had left the company weeks after I got there but was still friends with Chase, knocked at the door with what Chase later told me was a doctor's bag full of drugs, which everyone politely declined. Standard methods of being bad, like doing drugs, seemed inefficient and superfluous to us. The real drama was in the way we were changing everything, the way the whole world would relate to one another, so fast, without anyone knowing it yet. This, not actual drugs, was what got us high. For the rest of the night, I drifted in and out of sleep on the scratchy Persian rug, my feet occasionally accidentally kicking Justin or Emile, while Chase and Sean talked on and on.

On a hot May afternoon, a few weeks later, I was sitting in the back seat of Thrax's BMW, waiting for him to emerge from his apartment. Ariston, Thrax, and I were driving to San Francisco to see a band. Thrax finally came out of his building and walked to the car, slowly, because he was, of course, filming. He opened the car door and settled the camera on Ariston, whose beatifically wide smile stretched an inch wider for the camera. "Heyyy, Thrax," he said, almost flirtatiously. "Glad you brought that thing," referring to the camera. "Ha ha, of course, dude, of course," Thrax replied.

I noticed that when they were filming they spoke more intimately with one another. Perhaps it was because they were speaking not just to each other but to an audience that must be seduced. Technology was, as always, the alibi. But the camera didn't really protect them: It picked up every lilt in their voice, every tinge of desire. I suppose we must seduce our viewing audience because nobody came to Facebook to be unknown, uncelebrated, alone. They came to build something that would make them larger versions of themselves that would create fame and propagate it to everyone, everywhere. This was a new fame factory, and we were flirting not just with each other but with fame, with the idea that, someday, if we played our cards right, everyone would be watching.

Thrax turned the camera on me where I sat in the backseat. I was wearing my favorite terrycloth hoodie, which was almost a piece of armor at that point, a thin form of resistance to our new, constant state of video surveillance. My face was in shadow but my smile is bright, teeth gleaming digitally on the video that will live online forever. I declared to the camera, "Video nation," because that is what we were going to become. Facebook's user numbers were mounting quickly that April, reaching 20 million, our international networks were beginning to grow, and video would soon be launched. Thrax laughed with delight. "Video nation," he concurred, and cut the scene.

CHAPTER 6

THE MIRAGE

*F*acebook is a technical company," Mark began saying with increasing frequency at All Hands meetings in the spring of 2007, as we prepared for a new wave of product launches. It was a mantra that he wanted us all to memorize and repeat as often as possible to anyone who would listen. At first, I wondered what the force of this insistence was: why *technical,* and not *social*? If the product was about people, why was it important to say *technical* over and over?

Talking to various engineers about this, I discovered that Mark's point was to differentiate Facebook from other web companies for purposes of recruiting. "Good engineers will only work at a company that grants privileges to the technical people," they explained. "They need to know that their ideas and decisions will be considered primary, and not those of marketing or business guys." The unmentioned competitor in this conversation was MySpace, which, in March 2007, had more than one hundred million users to Facebook's 20 million but, nevertheless, remained an object of scorn. In the technical world, MySpace was considered a mere shell for spam, a skeleton social network built by an email marketing company rather than an engineering company. Because its parent company, Intermix Media, was based in Los Angeles, MySpace initially gained traction among aspiring Hollywood actors and musicians, thus cloaking it temporarily in an aura of artistic cool, but it did very little to develop itself as a product after that point. Thus, MySpace was not technical, and Facebook was. As far as Mark was concerned, Facebook was the first social network devoted to technology first, and he wanted to stake this claim within the tech community. Thus, Facebook planned and arranged its first F8 conference in downtown San Francisco, which was where Facebook would publicly announce its commitment to technology.

As May 2007 approached, the company prepared furiously for F8. The proof of the company's technical nature, which would be unveiled at F8, was the Facebook Platform, a new product or set of tools that would permit a Web application like Facebook to interface with external code written by outside developers. This would enable engineers who were not employees to build applications that run on the site. Users could then interact with friends on the site in a wide range of applications beyond the ones, like Photos and Groups, which were created by Facebook.

We were all so aligned in our sense that Facebook would

dominate the world that none of us really questioned the hubris involved in naming our conference "Fate." Platforms are the ultimate technology for a Web site with global ambitions because they are a way of bringing every developer to play on your turf, even if they aren't playing on your company's team, and we were the first social network to build one. Moreover, as far as Facebook was concerned, we were the first social network committed to technical innovation at all.

However, because I was not technical, I was not actually invited to attend F8, despite being employee number fifty-one at a company that now had over two hundred employees. In the push for technical dominance, Mark had been engaged throughout spring 2007 in a shift that a few women in the company began referring to as the "technical purge," in which everyone without a technical background suddenly found their positions in question. Mark began to insist that new positions be occupied by technical people. I wasn't particularly surprised, since, as customer-support employees, we always had questionable status anyway.

The customer-support reps who wanted to go to F8 could only attend on the condition that they serve as coat checkers. Perhaps I was as guilty as the engineers of feeling starworthy and VIP, but I wouldn't accept being treated like the second-class help, and this would serve me well. While the engineers were huddled in a room at San Francisco's W Hotel, where they could concentrate away from the crowds of press and developers swarming the conference, furiously preparing for F8, I left the Bay Area to spend the weekend with my parents in Huntington Beach. At the beach house my parents rented, I had to sleep on the couch, but it was better than checking coats at a conference called "Fate."

The following weekend, I was lying on a futon in Thrax's apartment late one night, listening to Sam, Justin, and Emile rehash F8. Thrax told a story about the night of the conference, hours before the Facebook platform was announced. The engineers were all holed up at the W, coding as quickly as their fingers could type. The problem was that the revolutionary platform, which Mark had announced in his keynote with the words, "Today, together, we're gonna start a movement," wasn't ready. The boys were still writing code and patching bugs to make it work at all.

Even though Thrax and Ariston began building Facebook Video in defiance of Mark's orders (as Video gained traction in the company and all employees were using it, Mark came to accept it) it turned out to be a boon, as it gave him a Facebook application built on the platform to announce as part of the launch. But at the eleventh hour, the platform and video were still unfinished, so even as Mark announced them, Thrax was writing furiously to code. As he told us the story, he had been coding for three days, and his body and vision were starting to fail. When he fixed the last bug to make video work, he left his laptop on the bed and went to the bathroom to get a glass of water. He didn't make it to the sink. He collapsed on the marble floor, exhausted, and fell asleep. Later he woke up and, in a half-dreaming state, tried to move but couldn't. His exhaustion was so extreme that his limbs couldn't register his thoughts. "It was scary," he remembered, "it was like my body wouldn't ever work again."

As the guys reminisced excitedly about the heroics of F8, congratulating themselves on their latest victory in the march to take over the world, I thought about Thrax's story. It was as if, in the process of building out his technology, he had reached the technologists' desired state in which he no longer had a human body. If the scene had been a video—and, for once, it was not, for there was no one there to record Thrax's fall—Daft Punk's "Robot Rock" would have been playing. This, maybe, was Facebook's primal scene: The moment when technology consumed the body, reality, and what was left of the physical realm.

Bored with F8 and Platform chatter, which was all anyone at work had talked about for months, I suggested watching *The Wire*. Sam agreed and Thrax quickly downloaded the first episodes of season one from one of his many pirated media sites. A few minutes later, Mark and a few friends arrived at the apartment to hang out. Mark said that he wanted to play video games and, since even at that late hour of the night he was still the boss, we let him commandeer the television in the living room for video games while Sam, Thrax, and I retreated to Thrax's bedroom to talk. Eventually, Mark left and we wandered back out to the living room to make up songs on the electric piano.

It was close to three in the morning when I left the living room and went to the kitchen in search of eggs. Thrax always had eggs, if nothing else, in the fridge, and it seemed like a comforting sign of a domesticity that couldn't be coded away. I made sandwiches out of eggs and stale bread, as Thrax and Sam tinkered in the dark on the piano. It was just us here, now, without the crowds and Mark and the blogs and the excited worship of influential Silicon Valley tech bloggers like Robert Scoble, for whom the Facebook Platform was the next great technical revolution, at least until the next exciting new application or platform came along. The only reason I knew who Scoble was, and that he had been raving about the platform, was because I was accidentally there, watching and listening to the boys that occupied the center of it. As I buttered the bread slices and slid the fried eggs onto them I wondered if the world would ever care as much about any of this—being technical, building applications, making platforms, owning platforms—as Mark and Scoble and the rest of the Valley did, and where all of this was going to lead.

"Are you coming to Thrax's birthday party in Las Vegas?" Sam asked me over IM while we were both at work.

"I can't . . . it's going to be like five hundred dollars for one night with airfare and the club and hotel," I typed back.

"Jamie says that you have to go. We need you," Sam returned.

"I know, but I can't afford it. I make a third of what you guys make. If they want me to go, they're going to have to help."

"Okay, I'll talk to Jamie and see what he says," Sam said, switching to a different AIM window to talk to Jamie.

Later that day Sam messaged me with an answer.

"Jamie says they'll pay for the club. He doesn't seem to get why, though."

"Ugh, I don't get how they don't get how rich they are compared to everyone else. It's like they think everyone is a rich guy from Harvard."

"Well, what they don't realize is that you'll remember this." Sam was right, just as he usually was when it came to reading the idiosyncrasies of the social world we inhabited. While I tended to observe things quietly, Sam unabashedly posted mocking witticisms on the other boys' walls, making loving jokes of everything they held dear. This was Sam's brand, and he could get away with it because, as an engineer, he knew they needed him. He was also gay, and cute, and being both made him an asset to others rather than a source of competition for female attention.

"They want us around to spice things up," Sam once said to me at a party, as if we occupied the position of some kind of self-aware court jesters. Sometimes, when we made fun of the more staid engineers, they liked it because mockery was another form of attention. Other times, they didn't realize we were poking fun. For example, rather than remembering the names of all the latest smart-phone models that were released every week, we began calling smartphones "technologies," refusing to differentiate between all the different versions like the Bold, the Pearl, and the Curve, that were being released as fast as RIM (and, very soon, Apple, with its iPhone, which first went on sale in late June 2007) could make them. "Use your technology," we would say when we needed to call someone or get driving directions. Soon some of the other engineers were calling their phones "technologies," too, either not realizing or not caring that we were gently mocking their and the company's obsessions.

While I made no secret of the fact that I found technology

to be as silly as it sometimes could be useful, I knew that I was still expendable, especially in the age of the technical company and the purge. My thoughts about Sam's conversation about the upcoming Vegas trip with Jamie, which I kept to myself, had to do with the Harvard guys' paradoxical cluelessness about the very things that they claimed to know most about: money and power. Their success in life, achieved in their teens or earlier, blinded them, I suppose. They assumed everyone had the same chances in life, the same easy path to wealth, where knowing just a little more about gadgetry than everyone else went a very long way.

Despite the fact that I was the poorest guest invited to the birthday party (everyone else was an engineer) by millions of dollars, I agreed to buy a two-hundred-dollar, round-trip Southwest ticket to Las Vegas for one day of partying. I figured that I'd just drink cocktails beforehand at the hotel instead of throwing hundreds of dollars at bottle service. Not going to Vegas for Thrax's birthday wasn't really an option. I was the only girl who was considered one of the boys. They needed me there, a female presence, an anchor around which they could keep oriented and keep things from spinning wildly out of balance. I felt like we were always in danger of that, as if with a little nudge, the entire enterprise, social and business, could veer out of control, fast. We had too much power, and very few checks on that power.

One day, at around this time, one of the Harvard guys posted a screenshot in News Feed of a new application that he, Thrax, and Emile were developing. It was not an official Facebook application. It was intended to be released as a platform application, meaning that users could add the application to their profiles if they wanted to, but that they didn't have to. I could see from the screenshot that the application was called "Judgebook," and that its purpose was for Facebook users to rate female users on their appearance. The screenshot showed two women's Facebook profile pictures, set side by side, with a space for the viewer to input a score for each. The tagline of the app was, "Judgebook .com: never judge a {face}book by her cover," which hardly made any sense, but the photos side by side made clear what the words couldn't: This was a way for men on Facebook to explicitly judge women's looks and assign them a score. For what? I thought, but then I remembered that Mark's Facemash application, which predated Facebook as his first popular Harvard site, was based on the same concept. The difference was that to make Facemash Mark had to steal students' photographs from the Harvard servers (for which he was famously disciplined by the university administration), but in Judgebook's case, the photos were already there on Facebook, submitted by users themselves.

In another screenshot in the same album, the Harvard engineer posted a screenshot of the domain names he had purchased to host the application: Judgebook.com and Prettyorwitty.com. It was like Mark's comment at the barbecue about having to choose between a girl who looks like a model or is smart, all over again, only in web application form. You could either be pretty or you could be witty and, in either case, you would definitely be judged and scored and rated. It was at moments like these that I realized it was the great and twisted genius of Facebook for anyone who was interested in rating things constantly, as Mark and the engineers who made these types of applications seemed to love doing. Facebook made it possible for men to have endless photographs of women available for judging, and women simply by being on Facebook became fodder for the judging, like so many swimsuit models at a Miss America pageant. Because, with Judgebook, like all Facebook platform applications, women did not have to consent to have their photographs used by the application. The application would alight upon your data and feed it into its database whether you wanted to be judged or not.

Sometimes, that year, I got a sick feeling in my stomach that I didn't want this world in which we are all ranked virtually, by virtual strangers, on the basis of popularity and appearance. Even worse, I felt like I might not have a choice in the matter. I didn't want it to be like this: I wanted us to make things better, not worse, for humanity and, especially, for women. I thought that more information would be helpful, not realizing that *information* as defined by these engineers was not value free. There were different kinds of information that we could be exchanging and receiving but, instead, we were learning about how pretty people were and whether people liked them, and how much. The world the boys were building was as weighted against the less powerful as much as the analog one they seemed to want to disrupt and leave behind.

On a flat, dry Friday in July I boarded a Southwest flight to Las Vegas for Thrax's birthday, happy as always to escape Palo Alto, if only for one night. I didn't care that I was about to spend my last five hundred dollars for what was basically a bachelor party without the wedding. I had been teetering financially for so long that this kind of budgetary risk just seemed normal. Besides, the cult of money and power that we belonged to was only getting deeper and bigger. I may have only had five hundred dollars in the bank, but there was an iceberg of money building under us all in the form of the stock options that we were all vesting month by month. The stock options still had very little value, as there was no public market for them yet, but, by May 2007, the site had grown past 24 million users, had 40 billion page views per month, and was already the sixth-most-trafficked site in the United States. As Facebook's potential to IPO became steadily more secure, though we knew it would be years off, it felt a little like we were all fronts for something else, faces of some future that hadn't yet been realized.

The year before, when Thrax and Sam and I had played at being high rollers at the dinner table at the Palms, it all felt adorable and twee, a grand lark, like we were Silicon Valley's version of starlets about to get discovered. Now I wasn't sure; things were more serious, less playful, heavier than before. Facebook was growing steadily bigger, but my doubts about the new digital world we were all beginning to live in were growing too. But, regardless of how I felt about the big picture, I had been at Facebook long enough, almost two years, that I knew I too had to win, regardless of what it cost.

A man sitting next to me on the plane took my mind off my brooding by buying me a gin and tonic from the always cheerful Southwest flight attendants, whose jokes on the PA system became bawdier the closer we got to Las Vegas. We toasted to the fact that in an hour we'd land at McCarran Airport, the gateway for so many unrepentant sinners longing for release into Las Vegas's bacchanalian excess. As we sipped our drinks and watched the red desert pass by underneath us, he told me about his job at a company in San Jose, which manufactured the security keys that we used to authenticate ourselves when we administered Facebook. In a way, we were in the same business: His job was to authenticate my employee identity, and my job was to authenticate his social identity. In the Internet's turn from anarchy to being a proxy version of real life, authentication was becoming big business.

The plane landed and we were released into the temple of tackiness that is the mirrored McCarran airport and the city it serves. The first blast of heat on leaving the terminal was liberating, soaking into my skin with an intensity that both awakened and calmed me. In the taxi line, I ran into a business development guy from Facebook whose movie-star good looks were widely considered to be the reason that he was hired, perhaps in addition to his Stanford MBA and whatever actual smarts he had. He was also there for the party, so we shared a cab to the Mirage Hotel and Casino. While he checked us in at the hotel desk, I stood on the busy carpet and watched enormous fish swim in the floor-to-ceiling tanks that line the lobby. As the fish watched me from the water I was not sure if I could tell the difference between observer and observed.

The view of the strip as we entered the penthouse suite the engineers had reserved for the party was breathtakingly bright and dark at the same time. Floor-to-ceiling windows gave onto an endless desert night punctuated by glittering signs that barely penetrated the blackness. The penthouse was entirely covered in marble, so it was like walking in a mausoleum. Sam and I retreated to the bathroom and took photographs of ourselves splayed suggestively against the tub. When we would get back to Palo Alto we would post them to the Facebook group we had made devoted to homegrown Erotic Photo Hunt pictures, as in the bar game where you look at two pictures of a lightly clothed person and try to find five differences. We created pictures for the group by first posing for a picture, then taking another picture in the exact same pose, but with a piece of fabric slightly moved, making a game of teasing the viewer. These tame Erotic Photo Hunt pictures were the premeditated, ironic version of the suggestive party photos that our colleagues posted on Facebook at the end of every weekend.

The mirrors lining all the walls of the bathroom multiplied everything, extending us to infinity, adding to the hallucinatory feeling that all of Las Vegas is designed to trigger. When we emerged from the bathroom, the penthouse had filled with friends, or rather coworkers, preparing for the party, dressed uniformly in collared shirts and skinny blazers. People brought bottles of liquor and lined them on the bar, like a movie about a birthday party in a suite in Las Vegas.

Everyone left for dinner except Sam and me, who remained in the suite like kids at an emptied-out grown-ups' party. The boys were going someplace expensive that I couldn't afford and, like the good friend he is, Sam skipped dinner and stayed behind with me. We turned the radio up loud and blasted the Cure, singing aloud to the sky and the lights twinkling for miles in the distance. "Love cats," we sang, tiptoeing around on the marble, spinning in circles until we were dizzy and collapsed on the lacquered sofas with a view to the Mirage's pools thirty floors below.

Eventually we descended the elevators to the casino with the intention of finding the boys, but were distracted by everything else: the lights, the tinkling of coins in the slots, the crowds thronging the casino, going to and fro as if orchestrated by machines. Disoriented, we walked outside to breathe in the arid desert air, and kept walking, down the strip, farther and farther from the Mirage. We came to a towering old-time neon sign for the New Frontier Casino. "Closing night, July 14" it read. That was the next night. We had to go in.

The New Frontier was in a sorry state, barely hanging on until its slated demolition. The slot machines continued their relentless beat, tinkling and singing with the sound of fake coins, but the air was heavy with smoke and dread. We toured the casino floor and put a few dollars in the machines. A waitress, soon to be unemployed, brought us white Russians made of the harshest of vodkas. We chatted with a few security guards near the cage, where all the money was dispensed, who told us the casino would be demolished in a few days. I decided that I already missed the place even though it wasn't gone yet. As we were leaving to walk back toward the Mirage, I took a picture of the New Frontier's neon sign, which read, "Thanks for the good times."

By the time we got close to Caesars' Pure nightclub, where the others were, we could barely walk, not because we were half drunk, but because our feet were worn out from trekking down a few miles of Las Vegas concrete. I checked my phone and realized that the others had been texting us all night. Their texts grew less grammatical as, I imagine, they grew increasingly drunk. "Where are you?" they asked, and Sam and I texted back that we were outside Caesars, collapsed on a patch of grass next to a barely clothed Roman statue that gazed seductively at the Imperial Palace casino across the street. "Come, we need you" they texted, over and over. What did they mean, they need us? I wondered. They never said that. They had never needed us so badly before. They never needed anyone. As far as I could tell, our entire lives at Facebook and within the site itself were being reconstructed so that no one ever really needed each other, as all our needs for attention could be satisfied by whomever was on-line, chatting with us or viewing our updates and making comments. "Should we go?" Sam asked. "I don't want to," I replied, "they only want us because we aren't there."

We lay back on the grass for a while and let the twinkling sky descend upon us, bathing us in uneven light, bright for nighttime. When we tired of the outdoors, we returned to the penthouse. None of the guys had returned from the club so we realized with glee that the one bed in the suite was ours. We jumped in, and I picked up the phone to call room service to deliver us a large plate of grilled cheese sandwiches, charged to Jamie's room tab. After eating the sandwiches, we fell asleep under the crisp white comforter, our fingers still oily with grilled cheese. Later, as the light was dawning over the strip through the floor to ceiling windows, all the guys tromped in, in various stages of drunkenness, and fought for space on the bed and on every available soft surface. Realizing that we wouldn't be able to continue our luxurious sleep, Sam and I got up and walked down to the pool, where people were already starting to gather in bikinis and swim trunks. We lay out on the chaises and tanned, half asleep, until it was time to catch a cab back to McCarran and fly home.

That Sunday, after I'd slept off our long night, I logged in to Facebook to see an endless stream of videos that the boys had filmed at the club. In them, the boys were not chatting up or kissing girls they had met, as I had expected. Instead, they were performing an elaborate ritual only they would have the strange, cold vanity to invent, in which they would methodically chat up and reject girls that the bouncers had brought to their table. "Leave! You're not pretty enough!" one of them seemed to say over the din of the club as he shooed the girls away in succession like so many servants.

Even though I had been living in this boys' world for almost two years, I was still a bit shocked. Their products ultimately reflected their real-life behavior. Instead of making a technology of understanding, we seemed sometimes to be making a technology of the opposite: pure, dehumanizing objectification. We were optimizing ways to judge and use and dispose of people, without having to consider their feelings, or that they had feelings at all.

What would happen to me? I wondered. Was I pretty enough to make it past the bouncers? Was that, in the end, what this was about? Was it even possible to be pretty enough? Were my colleagues ever satisfied with reality, or was reality always deficient in comparison to the perfected digital image? Did I even care? Did it matter if I was trying to win a war I didn't believe in? I wasn't sure, any more, what I believed in, but I knew that I didn't want to live in a world where I appeared only for a bunch of engineers to judge me and shoo me away.

In their minds, perhaps, the way this worked was that everyone who wasn't them was deficient. They were architecting a system that placed them on top. "I was born perfect," Thrax would say to me, in all honesty, the following year at Coachella, gazing down at his body as we lay around in bed, chastely as always. When he said it I, as I usually did upon hearing one of the boys' preposterous statements, laughed at the absurdity of his claim. What does being born perfect even mean? I didn't know, but perhaps your own perfection is what you would have to believe in if everyone else in the world isn't good enough. And that's why you'd want to reinvent a world in which everything had to appear perfect, all the time, as if forcing everyone else to believe in being perfect, too, or at least try. With my instinctive desire for authenticity and the slightly worn-out thing—the soon-to-close New Frontier—I didn't even know what perfection looked like. Perfect, to me, was the not perfect, the unfinished, the thing you loved because it had depth and edges and idiosyncrasies.

As I sat at my kitchen table in the Casa Real reading my News Feed and its exaltation of a boyishly cold, digitally perfected ego, I realized that I was furious at all this. I hate Judgebook, I hate rankings, I hate algorithms, I thought, in a moment of total rage at everything—the company, these boys—that was near, but also far beyond my control. I just wanted to be happy and loved for who I was and I wasn't sure all the algorithms or fame in the world could produce that.

CHAPTER 7

I'D RATHER BE CONQUERING

The Facebook Platform that was launched at F8 was, already within weeks and months of launch, winning. In fact, the platform grew exponentially overnight, to Mark's and many of the engineers' surprise and satisfaction. Application developers signed up by the thousands and built applications like Farmville and Scrabulous, as users' increasingly cluttered walls showed, soon gained wide distribution. By November 2007, over seven thousand applications had been created and each day a hundred new ones were being launched. In Mark's and some engineers' views, the rapid and unrestricted growth of the platform was good because it proved that at Facebook, technical development, not the desires of marketers or users, was king.

Not everyone was convinced that the rapid growth of the

platform was such a good thing: for the company, maybe; for the users, not necessarily. As customer-support reps, our job had always been to keep the site clean, monitoring for spam and aggression from individual users, doing our best to keep the virtual neighborhood tidy, and, we hoped, meaningful—a true "place for friends." We painstakingly and manually deleted accounts that we thought were fake, and warned people whom we thought were contacting users en masse, rather than communicating in a personal way. Though paid very little compared to the engineers, we were in a sense the defenders of authenticity on Facebook, at least until engineers could figure out a way to approximate our labor with algorithms, which they eventually did, to some user consternation as accounts came to be easily erroneously flagged and deleted.

But now, developers, who could sign up to develop on the Facebook Platform from all over the world, were pumping thousands of apps and millions of formulaic News Feed stories into our carefully walled and defended network. As far as external developers were concerned, the sole purpose of the platform was to generate more users for their app and, therefore, more money for themselves. In a sense, they were simply mirroring the engineering ideology of Facebook itself: Scaling and growth are everything, individuals and their experiences are secondary to what is necessary to maximize the system. Facebook, as we learned early in the case of the group titled "If this group gets 100,000 members my girlfriend will have a threesome," is the world's most efficient viral marketing platform, a way to turn automated word of mouth into gold.

The idea of providing developers with a massive platform for application promotion didn't exactly accord, I thought, with the site's stated mission of connecting people. To me, connection with another person required intention: They have to personally signal that they want to talk to me, and vice versa. Platform developers, though, went at human connection from a more automated angle: They churned out applications that promised to tell you who had a crush on you if you would just send an invitation to the application to all of your friends. The idea was that, after the application had a list of your contacts, it would begin the automated work of inquiring about people's interests and matching people who were interested in each other.

Soon, developers didn't even ask you if you wanted to send invitations to your friends. Simply adding the application would automatically notify all of your Facebook friends that you had added it and invite them to add it, too, using each user as a vessel through which invitations would flow, virally, without the user's consent. In this way, users' need for friendship and connection became a powerful engine of spam, as it already was with email and on the Internet long before Facebook. The same "We'll tell you who has a crush on you if you just send this email to your address book" ploys were familiar to me from Hopkins, when spammers could blanket the entire email server with such emails in a matter of hours, spread virally by students gullibly entering the names of their crushes and their crushes' email addresses.

When I first started working at Facebook, I wanted to believe that my experience there could have been a love story. That is, I thought, in some sense, that Facebook could be what we all—the employees, the users—sometimes wanted: A network through which we could connect and love each other more readily and more easily and with more permanence, a place in which we could feel more authentically ourselves, together, like every new model of social organization has attempted to engender since history can remember. However, as I gradually started to ascend the ranks that year, living in its virtual reality, I began to wonder whether to make a love story out of Facebook might be, despite our desire that it be so, impossible.

In some ways, Facebook's early years had all the makings of a bright, shimmering tale: an odd assortment of smart and dedicated people thrown together to try and figure out the parameters of a new platform, a better way for people to communicate. I wanted what I assumed everyone wanted: to bring people closer, to share important information faster, and to make everyone feel less alone. And, because most celebrated people at Facebook were, technically, if not intuitively, smart, and we all seemed to believe in the same things—in making something new—I thought it might work. I wanted the world to be better than before. I wanted to help people. If there was a big paycheck waiting for you at the end, I wanted it to be an incidental outcome of the revolutionary work we did together.

Now, two years in, I wasn't sure what was really happening with the burgeoning social media craze and its associated new forms of instant, distant interaction. What I was seeing was that social websites were playing upon the biggest open and unsolved wound in our society: the need to be known, the need to be loved. It was unclear if they were meeting this need. This need is so naked, so huge: In a society in which we are wage workers and paying customers more than we are members of a community, we yearn to be understood and loved for who we really are. We want people to see us, to care, to need us as we need them, to be there. But, more often than not, in our scattered communities of strip malls and subdivisions, they don't and they aren't. We move too much, and even when we are near, we are easily estranged, whether by work or leisure or now, technology, making it ever more possible to communicate without laying eyes on each other.

As Facebook and the social Internet grew ever bigger, I wondered whether what we were building was fixing our loneliness, or just becoming another addiction, like the social games that would soon begin to be pumped out by Zynga and others, that dull or distract us from deeper feeling. I was not sure if we were enabling love or its illusion.

In summer 2007, the launch and overnight success of the Facebook Platform, and the influx of cheap, viral applications it created, wasn't the only thing that was changing. By this point, the company had grown to almost three hundred employees. Most of these were engineers, in keeping with the site's philosophy of technical primacy, along with larger and larger numbers of customer-support employees hired to keep up with user growth. In June 2007, I was promoted to a customer-support training and quality manager, which meant that I was responsible for bringing new employees on board and teaching them all the ways of Facebook site administration. My promotion yielded me a raise to a salary that was about half what engineers were making on average, and a shiny new Facebook-purchased BlackBerry, which Andreas brought into my one-on-one meeting and pushed dramatically toward me across the desk, as if bestowing upon me some mystical, valuable gift direct from the king himself. I tried to act appropriately excited about the BlackBerry, but Andreas didn't know that Sam and I had been making skeptical fun of technologies and their talismanic quality in Silicon Valley for months. Skeptical or not, I would now have my own technology to consult at any moment.

Being on salary meant that I could be asked to work longer hours, so Andreas began scheduling me to come in on Saturdays to conduct intense training sessions with rookie customer-support representatives. At one of these Saturday morning sessions that summer, I was teaching the reps how to repair a Facebook account problem and I had my laptop projected onto the wall so everyone could see what I was doing on my screen. My instant-message client was on, and Thrax began a conversation, which, as they often tended to do, veered toward the topic of his penis. This was one of his favorite topics, in addition to anything digital, to discuss on Facebook and off with friends and coworkers. I quickly minimized the chat window and, after letting the reps out on a scheduled break, typed to Thrax, "I can't talk right now. I'm at work and this conversation is being projected." Only at Facebook, I thought, hoping the rookie reps hadn't read the conversation, but not feeling that bad about it if they did. They would get used to the work environment's weird and seamless mixing of personal and professional soon enough, I figured. At Facebook, to repurpose the old feminist saying, the personal was professional: You were neither expected nor allowed to leave your personal life at the door.

While I had become inured to (and sometimes enjoyed)

the antics that went on at work, I was still worried about what would become of me at the company. Teaching customer support wasn't the worst job, but it was far from a passion, and it continued to be frustrating to watch the engineers celebrate themselves and their increasing stature in the valley when I was still part of the lower caste, barely making ends meet. The dissonance that I felt daily flew in the face of what Silicon Valley says about itself—that it is a meritocracy, that it values intelligence and creativity, that everyone has a fair shot if they just work hard enough. This was true only if you were technical, and even that may not always be enough: In the age of the social network, who you knew and who your friends were became increasingly important, too. I decided to give myself a late August deadline: If there wasn't any movement in my career by that point, I would take my vested Facebook stock and strike a new path elsewhere, however difficult that might be.

I said as much to Thrax as we sat in the parking lot of Fry's Electronics on a Sunday morning. We had stayed up all night watching movies at Sam's house and then, after a walk around Palo Alto where we passed a church and toyed with the idea of going inside for the service (we decided against it, since we were dressed in jeans), decided to drive around. Driving around with engineers in Palo Alto almost always involved a trip to Fry's Electronics, so they could check out any new technical products that might have been released in the past week. I never minded going, because the store itself is a strange and fantastic monument to the Wild West. The aisles are decorated with bales of hay and statues of figures like Annie Oakley, who poses with a gun on a bale piled with Linux manuals. I could entertain myself for a good hour observing the Western decor while engineers poked around at newly released televisions and video games.

Back in the car, a Justin Timberlake song came on the radio and Thrax confessed that he liked it. Pale indie guys weren't supposed to like Justin Timberlake in 2007. "That's cool, I like Justin Timberlake, too," I said. In the same confessional spirit after our sleepless night, I added, "I applied to new jobs this week. I can't keep going in CS forever."

"Oh, no," Thrax said gravely, going silent for a minute as the Timberlake song finished on the radio. "You should be a product manager," he mused.

"Yeah, I know, but Mark doesn't want anyone who isn't technical to be in engineering anymore."

"Oh, right," he replied, knowing as I did that this decision, like anything else at Facebook, was only really up to Mark. In that sense, we were all just along for the ride.

"Whatever, let's go to In-N-Out," I said. When all else failed, in California, you could count on a good animal-style, protein-style grilled cheese (my usual In-N-Out order) to make things feel, at least momentarily, better.

"I tell everyone I meet that I can read their entire lives in one minute," Chamath Palihapitaya said by way of introducing himself to Facebook employees when he was hired as vice president of product marketing and operations in July 2007. He was a high-stakes poker player and ex-AOL Instant Message executive Mark was bringing on board, it was surmised by the tech press, to inject some much-needed business savvy into the organization. Chamath was young, brash, and masculine in style but, unlike most Facebook engineers, he had experience managing a company.

For his first couple of months, Chamath observed operations and interviewed employees to find out how things worked. My meeting with him came in early August. We met at Coupa Café on Palo Alto's Emerson Street, where laptops sat on every table and startups were the topic of most every conversation. Over cappuccino, Chamath asked me to tell him everything about my department. I told him who I thought did the bulk of the management work (certain members of the staff), and who didn't (our boss), and what I thought the issues in the department and the company were.

"We need to get you out of the department as soon as possible," he told me. "I think I have an idea of where you will fit," he said, but he didn't tell me where. I was elated; perhaps the technical purge was ending and Mark was finally open to the idea of creating meaningful roles for nontechnical employees.

The next week, Chamath asked me and my management colleagues in customer support to do an evaluation exercise in which we ranked everyone on the Customer Support Team from highest to lowest. Sitting up late that night in the office, I assigned a score to each person on the team. Some were easy to score: They were either spectacularly hard workers or rather lazy, preferring to play company-sponsored Beirut games to the alternately hard and tedious work of solving user problems, but for most it was a queasy and difficult process of comparing apples to oranges, which, in this case, might be one person's quickness at answering emails versus another's thoroughness and accuracy.

When the results were in, Chamath came back to deliver a speech. "Look around you," he told us. "In a few weeks, some of the people in this room won't be here. They will be moved to other departments, because they've worked hard and have made themselves valuable to the company. Other people in this room won't be here, because they haven't worked hard enough. I'm telling you this because you need to understand that this is how it works: You are always being ranked, and it's your job to perform. How you do here is up to you, but no one's going to let you get away with not pulling your weight."

One of the subtexts of Chamath's speech was that he and the powers that be had finally figured out that Andreas wasn't doing much at all and, though it took some months, he was eventually let go, to most of the customer-support employees' great relief. By then, I was no longer a member of customer support, so Andreas' departure was of only symbolic consequence.

Chamath had created a small platform product marketing team to promote the Facebook Platform to developers. The team was headed by Dave, a marketing guy who had come to Facebook in late 2006 from Apple, and a classmate of the early Harvard engineers, Eila, who had worked with some of them at Microsoft. She had a stunning command of business jargon: "Leverage, fire drill, best practices, deliverables" were a few of the words she used often and that I had to learn quickly. I was assigned to work with her on various projects, like redesigning the developer site (where external developers obtained technical updates about the platform) and reaching out to developers and encouraging them to build Facebook applications.

My first week in the job I was working at my new desk in

a cramped wing on the third floor of the 156 University office, where a jumble of database engineers and platform-marketing people sat, when I received an AIM from Thrax.

"Do you want to go to a show in Berkeley with us?"

"I can't, I have to work on a sketch for what the new developer site will look like," I typed back.

"Huh? Why? That's not part of CS," came his quick response.

"Chamath is my new boss," I typed.

"Chamath is? What happened to Andreas? Are you still going to deal with CS?"

"No."

"Oh, man. So you finally got what you wanted."

"Yes."

"Without resorting to quitting."

"Uh huh," I replied, waiting to be congratulated on my promotion.

"So, you're going to sit on our floor now? Lame."

"You're lame."

"Well nobody likes u so . . ." he typed, trolling. One of the engineering managers had once said to me, apropos of nothing, "Everyone likes you," with a kind of curious envy, as if this was the *ne plus ultra* of life for the Facebook employee. Facebook did not have the like button yet, but given that we soon would, being liked by everyone was maybe a form of ultimate Facebook victory. I was nonplussed by all this, still accustomed to the academic world in which being liked was suspect: It meant you might be pandering to people for their affection. But I figured that if being liked by everyone was an asset at Facebook, I might as well claim it.

Thrax and Sam and Justin drove off to Berkeley while I sat at work with my computer and a design program that I barely knew how to use, but I was in good spirits. Now that I had what Silicon Valley considered to be a real job, I thought, I could turn my attention away from simply getting along at the company to accomplishing something important.

As a member of the tiny platform-marketing team that Chamath assembled, I attended hours-long meetings about marketing strategy and slaved over my sketches for the developer site. The site deployed robotic, techno-style fonts and spoke exclusively in the language of growth and speed, the language of developers, unlike the user support pages that spoke of connecting to friends. The change from serving users to serving developers was interesting: Suddenly, I had switched from telling users what they couldn't do to telling developers that they could do anything they wanted. Facebook engineers considered the developers to be peers, so they were keen to make sure that we were communicating and on good terms with them, a concern they had never had with the users.

My career upgrade from dungeon department to quasi-technical role meant, along with a better salary and more respect from the technical echelon of the company, that I was now on engineering time. This meant that while I could come to work later, as late as lunchtime, I was expected to stay up until all hours answering emails and devoting myself even more monastically to our new enterprise. However, even as the respect and pay were higher, which was a huge relief, genuflecting to external application developers, even if I didn't agree with what they were doing, felt a lot like the eternal reverence we nontechnical employees were all expected to exhibit for Mark and the engineering department.

We arranged parties for developers on a frequent basis, arranged contests for them to compete with one another, and most important, looked away from the fact that almost all of Facebook users' data was available to them through the platform. Technically, they were supposed to scrub their servers of the data every twenty-four hours but, if they didn't, we had no way of knowing. Mark implicitly trusted developers, external and internal, as if programming web applications was a global fraternity to which one gained membership by writing code.

That December, after I had worked for four straight months without a break on the Developer site, an engineering manager, Kai, asked me in an email, "Would you rather work on Platform or help with the internationalization process?" Kai was an engineering manager who had previously held a pre-IPO position at PayPal and relished his role as Silicon Valley elder, though he was still young, barely thirty. He prided himself as much on his personality as his technical skills, trolling often on the company's social email list and generally behaving like as much of a character as possible. He had steeped himself in Internet culture since college. When he and his wife began to have children, they nicknamed them after Internet memes like the lolcat holiday, Caturday.

"Hmm, I'll have to think for a moment," I replied.

"As the Taoist philosopher Lao-Tse said, all decisions can be made in the span of one breath," Kai wrote back.

I knew immediately what I wanted to do, but I held back for a day or two just to gut-check my feelings. After thinking it through, the answer was as obvious as on first consideration: I loved traveling, I loved languages, and I had already taken the initiative with Sam to extend Facebook networks to foreign countries before site translation was even a twinkle in Mark's eye. Internationalization—the process of translating the Facebook site interface into different languages so that anyone in any country could use the site as easily as English speakers currently did—was what a recruiter might call a core competency of mine, even if I didn't know exactly what the translation process would entail.

I told Kai that I was game to transfer to the internationalization team and, when I returned from the holiday break in January 2008, I began the process of moving to the brand-new engineering office that had just opened in a building down the street from 156 University. The "i18n Team," as it was called ("i18n" was shorthand for "internationalization"), was assembled quietly, behind the scenes, by Kai. He embraced the brewing celebritization of Silicon Valley with gusto. Sometimes he would refer to himself and his wife as the "Brangelina of Silicon Valley." His passion for Hollywoodizing things extended to work issues: When presented with conflicts between team members, he cheerfully cited his wife's lesson in screenwriting class that all screenplays have a beginning, a fall, and a resolution. He would declare that the conflict was the fall and that we simply needed to work toward the narrative resolution in which all was resolved.

"Just do whatever you think would help get things started," Kai told me in one of our first meetings, with the relaxed management style that he made into a hallmark of his brand. His zen approach reflected the cherished valley idea that we, the employees of a successful startup, were all so brilliant that we already knew what to do and if we didn't, we knew how to figure it out.

In order to put me, a nonengineer, finally, in the coveted, unscripted position of doing whatever I think needs to be done, it was necessary to create a position for me on the engineering team, the site of all creativity in Silicon Valley. The newly created position didn't even have a name. "What would you like to be called?" asked my newly hired manager, a distinguished-looking older man with friendly, twinkling eyes, Hassin, who reported to Kai. He was a localization ringer from eBay, who had been in the translation business a long time. *Localization* is the industry term for internationalization and is thought to be more sensitive to non-US countries, since, unlike *internationalization,* it doesn't imply that the United States is the center. Alas, the term never seemed to stick at Facebook, as our team had already called itself the i18n team. I decided on internationalization product manager, since product manager seemed to be the term that, for the few women in engineering, was both authorizing (working with product was the highest status role Facebook had) and nonthreatening (it made no claim to actually engineer anything, so the engineers' technical sovereignty remained untouched).

I was finally in the driver's seat, in the engineering office, the place where the boys raced around on ripstiks and ran the entire show: Facebook, social networking, and the new social media industry. The freewheeling, fecund world of engineering was kind of its own self-fulfilling prophecy: When you were an engineer, you could make things be any way you wanted them to be.

"Welcome to engineering!" Mark's admin instant messaged me as I was getting set up at my new desk, with a smiley face tacked on. It did feel a bit like being handed the keys to the kingdom.

Getting Facebook translated into languages other than English was an obvious move, and the need to extend the network to the world was something I always believed in. The best and most natural use of the product's virtual scrapbooking had always seemed to me to be keeping up with good friends who lived in distant places. When you were living near your friends, seeing them seemed like a better option for keeping in touch than posting on a social network but, when you were living far apart, a social network could always help you stay up to date.

Unlike the Platform management role with its schmoozy developer politics, I felt no qualms about working on translation. For one thing, I was finally able to work on the real Facebook product for the purposes of serving all of the users, as opposed to serving only developers. Developing the Facebook product, which, by January 2008, 60 million people were using, was what engineers lived for. When you advanced or created a feature and launched it, one minute there would be nothing, and the next minute there would be something, a new Facebook interface ready to receive new users, their data, and their relationships to each other. I had spent too much time with engineers, seeing their excitement and thrill at launching new features, not to want my own taste of the creation moment. Thrax had joked one night to Sam and me as we prepared to launch international school networks in the fall of 2006, "Are you excited to spread your seed?" I guess we were. Each new network did feel like a product of our loins, there for our decision to lend it life, that night.

The best moments at Facebook always had this intensely potent feel to them: the power to create a world. I knew that feeling of power because, in launching schools, I felt it too. Once a new network was live, I would log in as "The Creator," the name of our omnipotent test account, to survey our new territory and poke around at the profiles of people joining it. Sometimes, when we logged in, we would update The Creator's status in words that we imagined the god of Facebook might post. One night I saw that The Creator's status had been set to "conquering," and I mentioned it to Thrax over IM. "Is The Creator's status still set to 'conquering'?" Thrax, who had posted the status, asked. "The Creator's status is always set to conquering," I answered. "Ha ha," he typed back.

Becoming a fully fledged member of the engineering team that winter felt, as I long dreamed of doing, like going from being slave to being conqueror. Suddenly, I could arrive at work on my own time, as long as I was working late into the night, because it was assumed that I, like all the engineers, was upholding and advancing a whole new world, even if sometimes we were just sitting around in the office eating snacks and playing games. In engineering, getting to work late was cool, even necessary. It meant, in the ideology of the lone and maverick hacker, that you weren't beholden to authority, and that you might have been up late coding something brilliant and life-changing and disruptive (even if you were just trolling Facebook or watching porn).

Being in engineering wasn't an escape from the game so much as the ultimate playground.

The new engineering office we moved to in January 2008 seemed designed to physically reflect that we were hovering atop the world, manipulating it digitally from above. It occupied the top two floors of a 1960s style office building in downtown Palo Alto. The floors had been stripped and customized to the tastes of Facebook engineers. The floors were a hard bamboo, the better for ripstiking on, and the walls were a stark white accented by primary colors of blue and red. (Apparently, Facebook's original graffiti artist, David Choe, wasn't available to paint before we moved in.) The desks were arranged around the perimeter of the floor so that a de facto racetrack looped in a long, unbroken oval around the office. There was almost always someone ripstiking on the track, making for a constant sound of wheels on wood and the regular, rhythmic appearance of nearly identical-looking guys in hoodies rolling past my workspace; it was almost like working in the middle of an eighties roller rink, without the big roller skates and even bigger hair.

The kitchens occupied a large section of each floor, but they were intended for snacking, not cooking (the only cooking device was a microwave). The walls of each kitchen were stacked with bins of every conceivable candy bar and cereal. None of the food seemed like food to me; it was all cased in plastic and preserved to eternity by chemicals that I couldn't spell, so I made tea instead and snacked on treats from the Japanese pastry shop down the street. I eventually asked if we could receive weekly deliveries of fresh fruit and gourmet cheese and of course, now that I was a product manager, my wish was granted. The engineers didn't always eat the fruit and it would often go bad, but I was relieved that the fruit—something organic—was there. It was the only organic matter in an office piled high with every kind of digital device anyone could think of to buy. (Some were provided free: A cabinet on each floor contained every possible technology, from adapters to storage disks to high-end headphones, that we might need to use in our work.) As I watched the delivery men cart crates full of pears and grapes into the office, I felt like I was trolling the boys with fruit, as if in delayed response to Thrax for making fun of me for looking for organic produce in Safeway.

Amidst all the troll wars and ripstik races that went on in engineering, there was still real work to do. Our task on the internationalization team was to get the site interface translated into as many languages as possible, as quickly as possible. We began the translation process with an idea for an application (which, like most Silicon Valley ideas, was a transmogrification of existing concepts, one of which was the news discussion site Reddit's voting apparatus) through which users could translate bits of text (called *strings,* in engineering parlance) on the site into their language. The application fed strings to users and they entered the translation in a text box. Other users could vote the translation up or down. This type of crowdsourced interface is all over the Web now as a way of managing the Internet's increasingly heavy flow of content, but it was a newer interface then, exciting to engineers in its limitless possibilities for mechanization of things formerly considered subjective.

Voting on highly subjective content, such as the right way to phrase a complicated concept like poking or the wall, can pro-

duce more conflict than agreement. There was often no defini-
tively correct answer but, instead, many different interpretations
of a given word. For example, the Spanish translators wanted to
know if *wall* meant the side of a building or something more like
a bulletin board (the answer was the latter, though then there
were an array of different words for a bulletin board for translators to vote on and choose from). Usually, the voting results
produced passable translations, but when there was a translation
impasse, I noticed that some engineers placed an almost reli-
gious faith in the voting process, and seemed to feel threatened
by the idea that the algorithmically decided results might not be
perfect. "The voting will fix it," they said, like a mantra, as the
translations rolled in and vied for victory on the page.

The engineers were beside themselves with glee when the
French version of Facebook was translated literally overnight by
local users; however, having spent a year in a French school as
a child while my mother was on academic business in France,
even I knew that the translations, while they were certainly done
marvelously quickly, were not polished and correct enough to
launch. I argued to my team that some kind of human review
of the final product was needed. I just wanted to know, for sure,
that the translations made sense and were at least a proximate
version of the quality on the English site. Some people on my
seven-person team, composed of engineers, Hassin, and a business development guy from Spain by way of Stanford, grew
frustrated with my stubborn defense of human cognition over
algorithm, but I didn't much mind. Being the odd defender of
the value of the human was something that I was used to and
was, after all, sort of my job. In more ways than one, I was like

the humanist troll to the company's obsession with technologizing everything.

Hassin, a linguist rather than an engineer by trade, agreed that some human input would be worthwhile and so I worked with professional translators to review the site in our first non-English languages, French and Spanish. Once launched, a user would view the site in French or Spanish by toggling a button on the Facebook homepage that would switch the language of the interface (user-submitted content like comments and status updates would remain in whatever language the user wrote in). I spent days with the professional translators while they read through pages of translations and made corrections as needed. They were working by the hour, clocking out at six o'clock, and thought it strange that I seemed perennially online the entire week, answering chats, reading Facebook, talking with them, answering questions, and responding to emails at all hours. When they left the office at the end of the day, they were done until the next morning. That, in turn, seemed strange to me. I couldn't remember when the last time was that I wasn't within spitting distance of my computer and smart phone. As much as I had once made fun of the Facebook boys for staring at their phones more often than they looked up, I had become one of them.

We launched the Spanish version of Facebook in February 2008 and followed with French one month later. Both Facebook interfaces launched to good press and widespread adoption, as the site was programmed to appear immediately in French or Spanish when a user signed up or logged in from a country in which one of those languages was primarily spoken. We moved on from those languages to getting the site translated into German, Japanese, and Italian. French and Spanish came first because they addressed the largest number of potential users but, after that, we translated in order of the wealthiest countries. Internationalization, like everything else, follows the money.

This was where I got lucky, and where my job began to save me from my dry, tech-saturated Palo Alto existence in a new way. Because we were striving for authenticity as well as technical accuracy in translation, it didn't make sense to hire American speakers of Japanese and Italian to translate the site. We didn't want a version of Japanese spoken by someone who hadn't been in Japan for years and wasn't current with the local idiom. Instead, two months after I started working on the team, Hassin decided that I would fly to Tokyo first, to work with Japanese translators, then fly directly from there to Rome, to work with the Italians. I was getting paid to go on a trip around the world, first class. "That's a nice gig," my dad said after I told him I'd be out of the country for a month. "Yes, it is," I concurred, relieved and excited. My commitment to blanketing the world with our technology was going to save me from it. It is neat how life works this way: No system is complete; there is always a way out if you work hard enough at it. And sometimes, as it was in this case, the escape hatch can be fun.

Flying to Tokyo in late March 2008 felt like the fulfillment of every late-2000s American girl's fantasy, since so many of us had seen *Lost in Translation,* and been entranced by its images of familiar American actors ensconced in Japan's cool, alien calm. I toyed with the idea of staying at the Park Hyatt, the hotel featured in the movie, but, in my perennial quest for authenticity, I picked the Okura hotel near the embassies, which had been renovated over the years to look exactly as it did when it was built in 1964. The Okura is a modernist Japanese wonderland full of exquisitely square, lacquered tea tables, enormous windows, and perfect stillness. When I arrived, I realized I was the only person in the hotel over five foot eight, and the only American. I felt like a huge cartoon character, with ungainly height and Technicolor blue eyes, struggling to appear restrained and petite amid the dainty Japanese women in dress suits and surgical masks having tea in the lobby.

When Facebook executives traveled, they had an administrative assistant arrange their trip for them but, in the simple, under-the-radar style of our internationalization team, I had no secretary and made all my travel arrangements myself. Not knowing how to arrange a car service in a foreign country, I took the subway to the translation office every day, finding my way via the signs in English that corresponded to the ones full of beautiful but, to me illegible Japanese characters. The train was full of young Japanese workers in accessorized outfits playing on their phones. It seemed almost weird that Facebook would be coming to Japan to bring them technology; they already had so much. They can probably do things on their phones that I won't for years, I thought. This was why winning Japan was so important to the guys in the office: not because they cared about the Japanese in particular, but because we needed to conquer the best. It was the Normandy of technology wars and, oddly enough, I, the American girl who didn't really care about beating Japan at anything, was the advance force, bringing them something they may not even need.

As it turned out, simply launching Facebook in Japanese wasn't enough to get many users beyond those with existing ties to America on board the site. Japan had a strong recent history of anonymous social networks, like the native network Mixi, and Facebook's insistence on real names flew in the face of that. In early 2010, Facebook opened a Japanese engineering office to target the Japanese market specifically but, to date, the network remains relatively unadopted (at 9 percent penetration) compared to other countries worldwide. But, back in 2008, we had high hopes that we could succeed.

At night, I went upstairs to eat in the restaurant on the roof of the hotel, fifty stories up, looking out over Tokyo. I didn't know enough Japanese to leave the hotel for dinner, and feared that I'd get lost. Gazing across the glittering city, I felt disoriented by Tokyo's size and its residents' calm acceptance that the city appears to go up and outward forever. My meals would go on for hours, with chefs preparing course after course of shrimp and exotic fish and finely cut vegetables on the gleaming grill at the bar at which I sat. As I sipped on tiny cups of sake and grew increasingly full, I would think, "I've come a long way from the Riviera," remembering the down-at-the-heels hotel in Las Vegas with a view of a parking garage that was my first Facebook-sponsored trip. When the bill came, I hardly looked at it as I signed, knowing that, like Thrax on his search for the most expensive restaurant in town, I could now, finally, charge anything I wanted to.

The 'round-the-world trip was a strange mix of power and disorientation, as if I were poised on the next great turn into the unknown of the cycle that I had signed onto almost three years before. When I left Tokyo a week later, and flew directly to Rome, it was the day before my check landed in my bank account, so I didn't have enough money to get Euros to pay for a taxi to the city. Sitting on my suitcase with my BlackBerry dying, I searched the Web until I found instructions in English for a train from Fiumicino airport to the city center. I sighed with relief when I was sitting safely on the train, its heavy steel wheels rumbling loudly into the ancient heart of civilization.

Having been traveling for almost twenty-four hours, I was so eager to get to the hotel that I accidentally got off the train a stop early and ended up walking the last blocks, trailing my suitcase along the dark cobblestoned street, exhausted and disheveled after a long flight during which the sun never set, allowing me to take photographs of Siberia that I later posted on Facebook. It was as if a part of me, childlike and overeager, still couldn't believe that I was doing this: flying around the world leading a charge for a company worth millions that would take over the world. At other times on that trip, I still felt like a kid alone in Europe with a backpack and not enough money to get to the next city.

However, once I was ensconced at what the Internet told me was the best hotel in Rome, I could relax, and took great pleasure in doing so. The room was small, as they are in Europe, but the walls were covered in baroque gold leaf and the bathroom was covered in black marble. I ordered room-service spaghetti from the Michelin-starred restaurant on the roof of the hotel and figured out how to order cars in advance to get anywhere I needed to go. It took a while to get the hang of it, but I was steadily learning how to play this business-trip game.

While Tokyo was interesting, Rome was, for me, much more comfortable, which made sense, for a million cultural reasons. There, in the musky villas of Italy, one of which housed the translation office where I worked with translators, was where the whole concept of conquering, and sociality, seemingly native to Italians, was invented (or at least that is what we were told in elementary history class). As I dressed each morning to take the car to the office, I felt like the female version of an ancient conqueror, intent on taking over Italy.

In my off hours, I ran around the city in gladiator sandals that would be perfectly in fashion when I showed up at Coachella two weeks later. Touring the Colosseum, I noticed a sign etched with a quote from Agricola that read, "The Romans, great robbers of the world, after all the lands have been devastated by their exploitation are exploiting the sea. They cannot get enough of East or West; they alone desire to possess with equal madness the richness and misery of nations." I took a picture and uploaded it to Facebook. Ironically or not—I couldn't tell anymore. At this midpoint in my career, I was on a mission to conquer the world, and the words resonated. That afternoon (which was the middle of the night in Palo Alto and prime engineering work hours), Thrax reached out to me, over AIM:

"Where in the world is Kate?"—thrax96
"I'm in Rome, conquering."—k8che
"I'm at my desk, conquering."—thrax96

I supposed then that we were both right, and whatever earlier misgivings I held about conquering it still felt exciting to be the bearers of this new world. That evening at Harry's Bar on Via Veneto, a luxe-styled vintage expatriate hangout with copious velvet drapes and tassels, I made sure to toast to our exploits. "To conquering," I said with a slight tip of the glass towards the Colosseum, never quite sure, as one can never be sure on the Internet, in its flat tones and wide openness to interpretation, whether I was half-mocking anything, including myself.

After a week and a half in Rome, working late nights and then the next day until dusk, taking a break in the early evening to drink Americano aperitifs on the Via Veneto and watch the passersby, I was ready and happy to return to the United States. In truth, I felt a new sense of victory and accomplishment after years of struggle and a sense that nothing was ever quite whole. In the previous three weeks, I had finished the Japanese and Italian Facebook, and even gotten a bit of a tan from walking around Rome. What's not to like? Facebook's cognitive dissonance was dissolving, for me at least: What they promised to the engineers, I—a woman, a nonengineer, a humanist, a writer—could have, too, and it could be fun. On my Air France flight back to Los Angeles, I thought of nothing but home: palm trees, sundresses, good Mexican food, the southwestern United States. Everything was finally coming together.

Even the fact that Air France lost my luggage on a layover at Charles de Gaulle Airport didn't ruin my bliss: It was April 24,

2008, time for Coachella again, and, as we had been saying on Facebook since 2005, I'm going to Coachella, bitches. In the only outfit I had, an ensemble that I had been wearing for at least thirty-six hours, I jumped into a rented Jeep and drove toward Palm Springs, in love with the desert dust, gritty and real, and the sun, bigger than it ever gets in northern California. The desert was my territory, prickly and warm and endlessly beautiful. Away from the thirty-inch monitors and endless nervous distraction of the Internet, I could live. I sang along to the bouncy Akon songs that played on the radio, more exuberant evidence that I was home in the United States, where our culture is hybrid and poppy, without history, perpetually new.

Since, as the logic of technology dictates, we must always be upgrading, Thrax had found a new house this year, bigger and grander than last year's, although there still weren't enough beds. It was a classic Palm Springs midcentury modern with a tennis court and a hot tub and at least three bedrooms. I hoped that I wouldn't have to sleep under the coffee table as I had the year before. But, after parking the Jeep in the driveway and entering the house, greeted by a mirrored wet bar already stocked with booze and backed by glass doors looking onto the pool and the desert, I didn't care anymore. I could sleep outside on the pool chaises if I had to: In the desert, I was home.

Later, sitting on the pool deck, taking in the huge purplish-blue sky, Thrax asked, sans camera for once, about my flight from Rome, not whether it was a good flight but what class I flew in. "Did you fly business class?" "Yep," I said. "Aw, yeah!" he cawed, "it's official!" In his eyes, my status at the company had finally been recognized. It was funny but not untrue, I guess, that flying business class, more than joining engineering, constituted proof that I had arrived. It was one thing for Facebook to ask me to get the site translated, it was another to buy me a nine-thousand-dollar plane ticket to Tokyo and another eight-thousand-dollar ticket to Rome and an eight-thousand-dollar return ticket to Los Angeles. The last month of my life—according to my travel receipts stashed away somewhere in my purse—cost Facebook more than my entire salary the year before. In Silicon Valley, you have to know that you are worth it to them, and money is the language they speak. Companies have *valuations,* as they are called, but so do employees, in the form of salary and perks and status, minute decisions made each day about where employees will sit and what they can get away with and what team they'll be on. It's simply that an employee's worth is not so explicitly stated by monetary value; it's all these things together.

As always, our days at Coachella passed like some kind of American Apparel–sponsored shaman journey that we shared with thirty thousand other people. The goal was to get from the car to the grounds to the sets we wanted to see, all without losing ourselves in the heat and the crowds. When, each night, we managed to find our way out of the trampled fields and to the car and home again we felt as if we had reached an oasis after a trek across the Sahara.

On Saturday night, we skipped the last headlining band and reached the parking lot early, having learned the year before that you have to have an escape plan. (In 2007 we didn't have one, so we had to hack our way out of the parking lot by finding a hole in the bushes big enough to drive through.) Our conversation in the car turned to how hungry we were and the fact that no one had eaten since our late breakfast at a roadside taco stand, so we turned off the highway in search of food, which is scarce in the desert at midnight. Soon, Thrax and I were in the grocery store again, only this time it was the Palm Springs Walmart instead of the Menlo Safeway. In 2008, even Walmart had an organic section, but I didn't care, because all we were doing was finding enough food to feed us after twelve hours of trekking across the Coachella lawn in search of music. I didn't argue with the hot dogs, sloppy joe mix, and white bread that Thrax dropped into the cart. My legs were wobbling with jet lag, and I was just trying to stay up and awake until we could get home.

In the checkout line, we leaned against the shopping cart, companionably close, hipbone grazing hipbone, too tired to talk. In my sun-worn and jet-lagged mind a vivid memory surfaced of us shopping family style at Safeway, two years before. Because Air France misplaced my luggage and I had yet to receive it, I was wearing Thrax's signature T-shirt, the one with a grenade on it and the name of the first streaming video Web site he made in Georgia, and madras camp shorts. "You look like Thrax," Emile had exclaimed with affectionate approval when I walked into the kitchen wearing Thrax's clothes that morning. As we walked down the checkout lane, Thrax pulled the cart behind him and I followed along with one hand on the cart, tired. "This is how my mom used to pull me along in the supermarket," he said, and in my boy's outfit I did feel a bit like the child to his parent. It wasn't the first time I felt like I was reverse aging into a pubescent boy, suffused by the postadolescent testosterone that saturates the office. "I'm just trying to make it family style,"

Thrax said, apropos of nothing, as if reading my mind, as the checkout clerk ushered us forward in line.

Oddly, Thrax often said something at the exact moment I thought it, as though our brains' synapses operated on some transparent wavelength, speaking to each other even when we weren't. Later on, when I was working directly for Mark and charged with the task of interpreting his thoughts for the world, Mark told me that his dream for Facebook was something like this, to make us all cells in a single organism, communicating automatically in spite of ourselves, perhaps without the need for intention or speech. Perhaps this connection with Thrax was some outcome of living in this new, technical Hotel California for so long, becoming attuned to each others' rhythms unconsciously, like female friends or coworkers who end up having the same menstrual cycle. Or perhaps it is something more archaic and personal. I no longer knew.

"Soul mates," Thrax said as we walked out of Walmart, speaking to himself and to me at the same time. I was so tired, still on Italian time, that it felt like I was living the line from *The Crying of Lot 49* that I picked for the "About Me" section of my profile, "Later, sometimes, she would have trouble sorting the night into real and dreamed." Was any of this real? What was I doing in a Walmart, in some boy from Georgia's grenade T-shirt, exhausted by world takeover? How could I be soul mates with a coworker that I would most often communicate with on AIM, like some disembodied voice from the Internet who only rarely appears in human form?

Soul mates seemed like such an odd word for Thrax to use that I continued to muse as we walked toward the car to meet the others, who had stayed behind. Connections, it had begun to seem, not a particular connection, are the point at Facebook and, through Silicon Valley's efforts, the thing that we are all connecting to was technology, not people. No one person, in the age of the social Internet, could provide the constant, easy attention that the technology can. As employees as well as users of Facebook, the work we did wasn't about focusing on one other person, or even on a few. Our job was to create a machine that attracted the attention of as many people as possible and allowed us to give it back in kind, and the only way it was possible to pay attention to that many people and be paid attention to is through technology. In real life, we didn't have that many inputs and outputs. We could only talk to so many people in a day. Technology, then, was our new soul mate, telling us it understands us, telling us that we are connected, that someone loves us, that we are not alone.

But then, I realized, Thrax might, as a human, have needed to identify a "soul mate" or two or three because the rest of his world was a chaos of technically enabled attention and infamy, a million races to beat others at this or that, in which a new race began as soon as the last one ended. In the constant chase after attention and fame, he might now more than ever need someone who didn't care who was winning, how many followers he had or what he had said online. Saying soul mates then, in our new world, wasn't about a real relationship but simply an assertion and desire for such a thing to exist, that there be some substrate of real beyond the screen, much like the sustenance in the form of sloppy joe mix that we had just bought at Walmart, that we must eat because, without it, regardless of how much we live in the digital world, we couldn't subsist. Perhaps one day soul mate, like friend, would be a category of Facebook relationship, content to be neither anything more, or anything less, than that.

A few weeks after my return, there were rumors of an important new hire that Mark had made to the executive team. That Friday, he convened an All Hands to introduce Sheryl Sandberg, a high-powered, multimillionaire advertising and operations executive from Google, whom Mark said he had been courting for an executive role since the Davos World Economic Forum in January. "Sheryl and I met at a party and we immediately hit it off," Mark announced. "We began talking for hours. She asked me questions about how I was running the company. I was really impressed with how smart she is." Mark spoke with an uncharacteristic smile and glow, not flirtatious exactly, perhaps a function of some kind of sense of relief, as if he had been seeking someone like Sheryl for some time. "When I met Sheryl the first thing I said was that she had really good skin," Mark continued, "and she does," he said, gesturing toward Sheryl, whose face was admittedly creamy in tone. She was smiling, and didn't flinch.

Sitting among my colleagues, I felt bemused and a bit perplexed, as I had never heard Mark comment on anyone's skin before. He obviously had never spoken about any of the engineers' skin as making them particularly suited to their role. Mark went on to say that, "Everyone should have a crush on Sheryl," and some engineers claimed in an engineering-wide email thread immediately after the meeting to have the requisite crushes. It seemed odd to me, as if all of this kneeling to worship Sheryl was some kind of compensation for the fact that no female employee had ever received such treatment before. At any rate, Sheryl had arrived, and would be occupying the role of chief operations officer. I wasn't sure what that implied at first, but it turned out to mean that she would handle everything that Mark didn't want to: essentially, all department operations outside engineering. In addition, with her Google ads background, she would have a prominent role in ads strategy.

At a one-on-one meeting with Sheryl weeks later, I found out that she had an interest in the topic of women at Facebook and in Silicon Valley generally. In her months-long process of getting to know the company, she scheduled individual meetings with all the women in engineering. (By that point, they numbered about fifteen out of hundreds of engineers, including Maryann, who had been promoted into a position as user experience lead on the engineering design team, and would eventually come to manage the user experience team, a new department that was devoted full time to testing new features and collecting user feedback.)

Sheryl and I met in a small meeting room off the mini-kitchen on the engineering floor. "I don't know if you know this, but I do a monthly women's meeting at my house that is women only, where women in the valley can gather and hear an interesting female speaker and talk with one another," she said, "so I care about this stuff." She paused for a moment. "Tell me everything," she said, directly, leaning forward on the couch where she sat. I liked her forthrightness and the way she looked at me directly, creamy skin and all.

I told her that I was generally happy in my role as internationalization PM, which I was. I also let her know that there were a few situations involving men in the department that I thought she should know about. For example, one of the engineering directors had been known to proposition women in the company for threesomes; I also had an issue with an engineer who behaved alternately dismissively and aggressively toward female product managers, but the situation had been handled ineffectively. "I was told by an engineering director to go in and talk to the guy and try to resolve the situation myself, but when I did that, the engineer somehow twisted things around and called me a bad feminist, as if to distract from the conversation at hand, and the conversation didn't go anywhere. It was pretty unpleasant," I said.

"Offense as defense, I get it," Sheryl commented.

"Yeah, exactly," I concurred. Sheryl is cool, I thought, she gets it.

"Well, thanks for talking to me, I really appreciate it," Sheryl said, winding up our conversation.

That was the last time I met privately with Sheryl, and I thought that if her conversations had gone similarly with other female employees then her arrival was definitely going to be a boon for women at the company. I didn't hear back immediately about any of the issues I had raised with her, until she stopped briefly by my desk one day a few months later and in the low, succinct office voice that she mastered, said, "I just want to know that the situations you told me about have both been handled." I had heard nothing about it. "You see, I'm so good that I make things happen and no one even knows about them," she smiled.

It was then that I noticed that the director who propositioned employees had been subtly demoted and the aggressive engineer had been transitioned to another team. Both men, of course, continued to work at the company, so in some sense I wasn't sure what exactly would be different. However, the fact that that there had been some action, after years of guys getting away with whatever behavior they wanted, was comfort enough.

Sheryl's housecleaning sweep through the department was the last transformation of our workplace that most of us saw from her, as far as our day-to-day work was concerned. Mark continued to conduct the All Hands meetings and serve as the voice and visionary of the company, which was his due, of course. However, women I talked to were disappointed that Sheryl and her voice had quickly receded to the background, leaving Mark and his vision of a brash, move fast/break things culture to define the company.

Aside from the initial excitement and activity surrounding Sheryl's arrival, as 2008 drew to a close, the office was crowded with more and more guys, in desks packed increasingly close together, but there were still very few women. Facebook had started to resemble, more than ever, a fully fledged fraternity. Sam even said so to me as he was telling me about some tournament—whether chess or ripstiking or gaming—the guys on our floor had held the night before. He liked the fraternity aspect of Facebook, to my initial surprise but, as I thought about it, I began to see why. These were the brothers he and all the boys never had, the popular techno frat that didn't exist at Harvard or Stanford. The engineers had been together so long that they knew each other inside and out, like frat boys in their senior year. They played games of chess all day on the kitchen tables, and didn't look up when I watched, as if they didn't see me, because they didn't; like any woman on the sidelines of a varsity match, I was not in the game. They raced ripstiks around the floor all day and night, keeping charts on the whiteboards of who won.

Their venture into a world of pure competition was here now, charted by points and what Facebook would soon call *credits,* a form of virtual Facebook currency that began to be tested internally as a way for Facebook users to reward each other for posting entertaining things. Winning battles for status was no longer the precocious activity of young hackers, but a codified way of life. And, just like in a real fraternity, there was an obvious hierarchy, as well as rituals, which in this case involved chess games and the occasional limo club night instead of football and pub nights. Facebook had made being a nerdy programmer cool and normal, at least within the confines of the valley.

I stopped paying attention to the social dynamics at work, since, like all frats, everything and everyone in it looked the same from the outside. I was a sorority of one, and it was getting lonely. Any hint of a new, creative, coed society that I had felt in the beginning, composed of gays and straights and men (or boys) and women, had become stratified and compartmentalized just like in the American institutions we had wanted to leave behind.

Fortunately, my job kept me traveling for the rest of the year, bringing me back to Palo Alto only long enough to get lonely again before I could pack for some new and exciting destination. I was in Dublin for work on September 29, 2008, when the stock market crashed, and I spent the night in a bar at the Four Seasons Hotel, reading news of the crash on my laptop as piano music tinkled in the background. While checking Facebook, I received an invitation to a group created by a designer called "Party like it's 1929," that bore the description "If we're going down, might as well go down in style."

That night, I also received an email that Dustin had sent to the engineering team announcing that he would soon be leaving Facebook to, as everyone always said when they left, pursue new things. Noooooooo, I broke immediately into a silent wail, my eyes tearing up, not quite realizing until that moment how much I had depended on Dustin to be the company's witty, practical, human counterpart to Mark. "Daddy Dustin," Sam and I had sometimes jokingly called him, since we all sensed that Dustin was the one most likely to listen to us if we had a problem, or needed to talk to someone in power. I ended the night by writing a Facebook message to Dustin to express my gratitude to him simply for having been there, though I had never called on him directly, then went to sleep in my hotel room as the lights of Dublin twinkled coldly in the night.

Whenever I landed in some city, fresh from business class and flush with my Facebook expense account, I had the precious experience of being anonymous, free, unlinked to a hierarchy that I didn't control. I started to revel in that freedom, purchased ironically by a site that would like to remove anonymity from everything. "In the future, when you check in to a hotel it will know what music you want to play and who your friends are, based on your Facebook profile," I used to tell people in my prior job as platform product marketing manager, to tout the possibilities of the platform and its promise that we could have our friends and our likes with us, at least virtually, all the time. But, in truth, I was almost happier escaping to places where no one knew me.

Several times, when I was not scheduled to make a business trip, I made the one-hour hop to Las Vegas for the night and checked into a hotel, in love with the glittering anonymity the city affords, the sense that no one on the Strip knows who anyone else is: There are too many people and too many nooks and crannies in all the casinos for anyone but the casinos' eyes in the sky to keep track of. Real friendship and intimacy are beautiful and necessary, I knew, but I was starting to wonder exactly who my friends were. Were they all the people on my profile, or was there some finer specification, and what was it? It was hard to tell anymore.

Back in the office, friends were an elastic, untroubled term. Many of the people on my Facebook profile were coworkers I interacted with on the site only, but, to most, there seemed to be no discrepancy in this. In the logic of our business, to comment on a friend's post was better than speaking to them, because everyone saw it. Everyone wanted to see everything. This was all justified under the company's corporate buzzword, *transparency*, though no one seemed to know exactly what it meant. The fact that it was hard to define led Mark to begin a discussion on the company's internal discussion page asking everyone to submit ideas for what *transparency* was. We discussed the word for days, and all that was decided was that no one knew. For some, like

Mark, who posted in the thread with everyone else, the word *transparency* seemed to have the ring of enforced integrity, as if in a transparent world there could be no lies, no hidden information, and that nothing bad could happen because everyone knew everything about everyone. I was not so sure. Having occupied a powerless role at Facebook, I was conscious of the way in which power affects behavior. The engineers acted; the support team and users were acted upon. This disparity was why, sometimes, revolutions had to happen, or at least percolate, anonymously and in secret.

The simplest definition of transparency that I figured applied to the context of Facebook was a sheer technical one, using technology to broadcast whatever was happening, a Big Brother by another name, but with what the company considered a positive value instead of a negative one. One Saturday in November, when I was in the office (weekends were the best time to work because it was the only time when the office was quiet and I could get anything done), I took a break to play Rock Band with Emile and Thrax in the glass-walled game room on our floor. They decided that it was not enough to simply play the game. Everyone needed to see us playing the game. They rigged a video camera that broadcast our performance onto the wall and also onto the Internet, where Emile and Thrax's legions of Internet fans were apparently waiting, ready to watch from their bedrooms in Croatia and Louisiana. They also rigged an input device so that the fans could talk to us. Their chats were broadcast onto the wall for us to see and respond to. We were as close as we could get to total transparency, a set of characters in a virtual world full of people watching and listening and talking with us from around the globe.

In the midst of banging out a version of Linkin Park's "Crawling" on our plastic instruments, a viewer typed "You are gay," at us, religiously following one of the Rules of the Internet, which is to always question someone's sexuality, for no reason. "Yes, I am gay," Thrax typed, following another rule of the Internet which is do not argue with trolls, if you do, they win. I felt a bit like Margaret Mead on Bali, watching the natives of a distant world enact their culture.

The fans watching us on the Internet were perplexed to see me there, since another rule of the Internet states that there are no girls on the Internet, and they proceeded from questioning my gender or even my existence, to telling me that they would like to fill all my holes. This was standard Internet behavior, and I barely blushed, though it seemed a bit violent, in a virtual way, much like the Internet itself. People will do and say anything online because they can. Thrax and Emile were unperturbed, barely registering the curse words flowing at us through the screens, since this was the way the Internet was. Not only were insults the Internet standard but, as Facebook grew, we were becoming the Internet, its new owners, like the rail men of 1880s America surveying their newly installed rail lines in the Wild West, kicking the iron and making sure it worked. And work, it did. Like the boys in their rooms in distant states, we were safe here five floors above Palo Alto, connected by wires to worlds we would never see.

Later that afternoon, I walked the few blocks home to my apartment. As I was cooking dinner, with my laptop open on the kitchen table, my screen was still tuned to the game room in the office, the boys were still playing, and the watchers were still watching, throwing insults and questions at the screen as Rock Band songs started and stopped, chords scrolling endlessly to infinity. I closed the laptop and drove to San Francisco to meet friends and go out, in real life.

San Francisco is a thirty-minute drive from Palo Alto, but every mile felt like it was taking me slightly closer to reality, or at the least, to some Bay Area approximation—now abuzz with Twitter and a whole new generation of social apps—of it, that I sorely needed. Like the old Facebook relationship status option that we removed some time in 2007 in order to make the site sound a bit more mature, when it came to reality, I was at a point where I would take whatever I could get.

CHAPTER 8

THE ♡3 ECONOMY

If, in 2006, Palo Alto felt like a shimmering, tech Disneyland, a city in circuit-board form, all tidy blocks and green lawns and the near-silent hum of every form of digital device anyone could think of, by 2009, it had started to feel like a shopping mall for venture capitalists searching for the next Facebook. New, glossy restaurants sprang up to serve unending rounds of business lunches; a Four Seasons Hotel went up at the intersection of University and the 101; all last traces of Palo Alto's scrappier preboom days were washed away, replaced by the town's brand of bland, midrange minimalism.

San Francisco, by contrast, was still a welcoming, disorderly mixture of tech wealth and street grime. When I went there on the weekends, I could only wear flat gray boots and tights under neutral skirts, because anything I wore emerged a dirty gray anyway, not unlike San Francisco's sky with its persistent fog punctuated by sun, and sun only on certain streets. For all the extremes of climate and class—you are as likely to be chased down the street by a bum demanding change as jostled on the sidewalk by a tech multimillionaire focused on his iPhone—San Francisco retains an aura of cool authenticity, the muscle memory of having been once a gritty gold-rush city, packed with drunken miners and the women who tended to their needs. Thus, people flock there from all around the Bay Area on weekends to soak up some remnant of a hearty, physical past, made edible in the form of rustic breads at Tartine, and whiskeys neat at the many bars along Mission or Valencia Street. Whatever San Francisco lacks in leftover grit, it can afford to invent in the form of endless dives (some truly old, some decorated to seem so), handcrafted cups of coffee that take five minutes to brew, and high-end restaurants decorated to look like 1800s homestead kitchens. However stylized, San Francisco is the unpolished flip side to Silicon Valley's perfect grid.

In contrast to the hardscrabble aesthetic emerging in the Mission, Facebook remained insistent on its high-tech fantasy of a perfected, digital life, where everything was always new and inefficiency was always being outmoded. "Harder better faster stronger," Daft Punk's robot vocals still looped in the office and at company parties, perennially picturing a cleaner, faster world. But Facebook's rapid growth, at 700 employees and 150 million users, strained at its uniform ideals. New offices full of Facebook lawyers, advertising managers, and User Operations (as the customer support staff were now called, in recognition of the fact that the department served users rather than paying customers) employees sprouted up around Palo Alto, staffed with people of all types, though the engineering office remained as concentrated with young men as ever. The company did its part to maintain a young aesthetic across the departments by issuing branded American Apparel T-shirts and sweatshirts. Other companies in Palo Alto issued their own branded clothing, making for humorous scenes where, say, a team of ten Palantir (another Peter Thiel–funded startup, this one devoted to developing software for military intelligence) engineers in company-branded track jackets faced off at a crosswalk against a team of engineers in the same jackets that said Facebook on the front.

By 2009, the once cool and spacious engineering floors, where boys could ripstik around freely at top speed, were growing crowded with desks, toys, and new engineers who were being hired as fast as they could be found. As the din in the office rose I kept my headphones on and my eyes glued to my screen, monitoring the translation process, my inbox, and my Facebook feed, in which boys took turns noting the failings of some new piece of technology or posting photos of the new devices they picked up that week at Fry's Electronics.

On Mondays, the albums full of party photos from the weekend would begin their march down the News Feed. Photo albums posted by Facebook employees had more so-called weight in my News Feed because they usually contained other Facebook employees, and the News Feed algorithm assumes that if many of your Facebook friends have done something, you want to know about it. The combined algorithmic weight of friends tagged in Facebook employee party photos and the sheer number of photos that they posted turned my News Feed into an endless panorama of coworkers socializing, perpetually frozen in smiles with drinks held to their chests. Their photos increased in visibility for the next few days of the week as fellow employees liked and commented on them. The people whose photos were liked most rose further in the rankings so that, the next week, I was more likely to see their pictures, whether or not I ever hung out with them. News Feed was, to my bemusement as a *Heathers* fan, like the algorithmic version of the Heathers in the cafeteria, taking note of whose popularity was rising and falling and making sure that everyone was apprised of the popular people's movements.

My monitor pulsed with a steady flow of emails and task notifications, some urgent, some not so much. An enduring argument on the engineering social email list about the best way to optimize the temperature on the engineering floors would include exchanges like, "We should vote on what temperature everyone wants it to be," and the reply, "No, then the result would be suboptimal for at least half the office." The arguments on email could go on for hours, circling around the logic of what was essentially subjective: room temperature. Subjectivity in general tended to drive engineers crazy: They wanted there to be one answer, one solution, one optimization that worked for everything. As often happens online, these threads devolved into an argument about the communication form itself: "Stop switching the headers on the subject lines," one engineer would command icily, "it ruins the threading in my inbox." "Stop sending so many emails to e-social, you're ruining my productivity," another would say. "No way, e-social is sacred," someone else might claim. "You're supposed to be able to send anything you want there. If we lose e-social, we lose our culture." In a pattern common to online communities, the social list began as a dream of easy, fraternal companionship, followed by a rising, fractious concern that the quality of its community was being lost.

Just as in earlier days, users fretted constantly that Facebook was becoming MySpace; as we grew, we fretted constantly that we were becoming not-Facebook. By 2009, everything that happened at work seemed to prompt the feeling that, in Facebook's perpetual nostalgia for its own early culture, we were losing our utopia. It was starting to always be the "end of an era," as the boys commented often and nostalgically when looking at old photos of themselves in the office: The boys were growing older despite themselves; the office was growing bigger despite Mark's desire that it stay small and focused. "Smaller companies are always better," he would say in All Hands meetings that year to explain hiring plans and why, even though we were growing quickly, he wanted to avoid uncontrolled hiring. Size was the enemy of swiftness, and swiftness: "Moving fast and breaking things"—was the company value that Mark repeated most often. (The others, like "be bold" and "be open," were less punchy and required more effort to explain.) As the engineering team grew into the hundreds, the product teams were refashioned on the model of little startups, with their own war rooms, so that they could feel like small companies despite being part of the larger group.

Despite all these attempts to remain small in feeling if not in reality, in meetings, almost daily, someone would say, "I am worried that we are losing our culture," and everyone would look around helpless, as if they didn't know what to do, or how to save the precious essence that they felt slipping from their grasp. Sitting on a meeting room couch, listening once again to this exchange, I recalled my Hopkins advisor saying, "You are what you do. If you don't do it anymore, how can it be your culture?" He was making a point about cultural identities in America and our constant fear of losing them, even when we don't practice them anymore. I came to realize it was the identity of a nineteen-year-old boy, forever youthful and reckless, unmonitored and unstoppable, that the boys were so anxious about losing. They were worried, perhaps, about growing up. *Facebook culture,* by another name, then, might be a fear of adulthood, a desire to put off commitment, responsibility, and the difficult work of relating in real life and in real terms, forever. But how do you save your youth? How do you stay nineteen forever?

In December 2008, I was tapped again to do a job that didn't exist before and didn't have a name. "We are looking for someone to write for Mark," Facebook's Communications Director Elliot Schrage, a public policy lawyer turned PR executive who came to Facebook from Google, told me. "We're going to send out the job opening to the company so anyone can apply, but I think you would be great for it." Lols, I thought, slipping into the emoticon talk that had begun to move off my screen and into my speech. I was, after all, the only writer there, or at least the only writer who had been at Facebook long enough to justify entrée into Mark's exclusive inner circle. In the past year, Mark's circle of confidants had thinned as his original cofounders, like Dustin, cashed out in the billions, and it had to be restocked.

This shouldn't be hard, I thought. I had been listening to Mark speak about product launches for three years, and I knew all his rhetorical tics and gestures, even if I was still not entirely sure what he truly wanted for the world, or what drove him, beyond a fascination with youthful insolence, ever-expanding territory, and control. His voice is a combination of efficient shorthand (no overly big words, no overly long sentences) and imperialist confidence, always gesturing toward the next stage of the product's growth, depicted as inexorable and unlimited. Things were always being "pushed forward" in Mark-speak, as if he and the company were Atlases simultaneously shouldering and spurring the world's advancement, moving it forward with their own digital might.

Just as in the Daft Punk song, in Mark's rhetoric, Facebook's work was never over. It wasn't a Web site or a set of apps, but a platform that grows and grows, adding more users and entities (brands, places, events) and going deeper into our lives, mining that data for the benefit of the platform and, he argues, all of us. Who wouldn't want to have easy access to everything, every person and place and event around the world? he wanted to know. For a second or more, as long as it takes to log in to our Facebook accounts and survey the world before us, we all say *yes*. We too want that. Who wouldn't? As the hackers who devote themselves to pirating know, free data is seductive, enticing. There is always more and better and newer data to obtain, and new and faster ways to acquire it.

Writing a blog post in Mark's words, then, would mean formulating sentences that sounded like they were coming from the master and commander of this global platform, someone who believed in it, and assumed that you believed in it and wanted it too. If I got the job, this would be a fun puzzle, not unlike the programs the boys wrote to obtain the data they wanted: how to think like Mark, how to convince everyone that Facebook is a necessary and inevitable world-changing thing, our world's only hope for true and permanent connectedness. I knew how to do this in part because, in my more enthused moments, I believed in it too.

I worked on a sample blog post for Mark, beginning with his standard "Hey Everyone" and proceeding to describe the ways in which some new feature advanced our Facebook-connected future. The work took an evening, punctuated by exasperated moments of typing and erasing and retyping, trying to get the boyish cadence just right: just flat enough to sound like Mark, but still animated enough to be readable, compelling.

A few days later, Mark asked to meet me in his conference room. It was my first one-on-one with the boss and the first time he had ever given me his full attention, even though at this point I had worked for him for over three years. His conference room was entirely white: white plastic Saarinen table, egg-shaped chairs, white walls, whiteboards. From the glass windows I could see as far as Stanford to the west and the peninsula to the north, like a long corridor of wealth stretching to the horizon, tapering off into clouds.

Mark closed the door and stood near his whiteboard, dressed in his usual outfit of squarely cut jeans and a hoodie, looking slightly away and off into the distance. Whenever he looked at me directly, which was rare, it was either with blankness or a slight smirk, some acknowledgement that we were in on some joke that he assumed that I, as longtime Facebook employee and member of what felt by now like a virtual family, would get. I wasn't sure what the joke was, if it even existed, or if our simply being there—in command of a universe—was the joke.

"How did you know how to write like me?" he asked with disbelief, once I had situated myself at the white table, my arms folded. "When I read this I thought it was something I wrote." A slight smile appeared on his face, finally. When he smiles, you know he feels comfortable, among bros, like you're at the fraternity house and someone has said something particularly funny. I have worked hard, I suddenly realized, to hone myself into a proxy bro to these boys: nonchalant, stolid, avoiding the appearance of caring too much about anything, but especially about the wrong things, which are anything too girly or nontechnical or decorative, things that in this world do not scale. All the girls who acted like girls (and who didn't have social connections to the founders and early engineers) were still stuck down in the lower tiers of the company, largely ignored except when they appeared at company parties or in the tagged photos of them that appear on Facebook after parties.

"I don't know, I guess I've just spent a long time listening to you speak."

"Okay, well, you've got the role," he announced. Facebook tended to refer to jobs, especially the loftier and more outward-facing ones, as "roles."

"Cool," I replied, "I'm excited." I was. My interest in internationalization had been waning since we had finished translating Facebook into nearly every language. By that point, my job had segued into managing the maintenance of the translated Facebook sites, which was a more bureaucratic function than the original translation process had been. Writing for Mark, on the other hand, appealed to a stronger passion of mine: writing in English. It might be the funniest thing I had ever done, and the weirdest job I'd ever have. It seemed almost perfect that I, fascinated by the dark sides of Facebook, would become the shadow Mark Zuckerberg, there to explain what he couldn't or wouldn't.

Mark took out the sample blog post I had written and made a few stylistic notes on it with a pen. "This pretty much sounds exactly like what I would write," he said. "Except for one important thing. I never use a comma before a conjunction," he said, crossing out all the Oxford commas I had inserted as a matter of habit.

"Okay, no Oxford commas," I said. I could already see why he wouldn't like them: Oxford commas weren't efficient. His style aimed towards the quick, modern, streamlined. I reminded myself also not to use two spaces after a period.

"Have you seen *The West Wing*?" he asked.

"Some episodes, yeah, but I've never watched the whole thing," I explained.

"I want you to watch it," he said.

"Okay," I agreed. Of course, *The Wire* was the show that I believed best reflected how things really work, at Facebook and anywhere else. But, where I saw the struggle, the war on the streets that wasn't polished and clean and was waged by people who weren't in power, Mark saw the presidency and some new virtual Oval Office of his own making, as white and spotless as his fifth floor conference room.

I wondered sometimes if the very fact that I saw things in ways he didn't was what had gotten me that far. Because, for all their rabid data consumption, there was a lot the engineers didn't know. That was partly why Mark made Facebook, and why the boys of the valley were so busy turning our lives into data, as if by doing so, their algorithms could tell them something that their eyes and hearts couldn't. As Thrax announced triumphantly at his desk one day, "I just wrote an algorithm to tell me who I am closest to!" He went on to show a set of scores that, according to his algorithm's calculations, revealed how close he was to all his Facebook friends.

Two weeks later, my job in internationalization wrapped up and, in my new role as Mark's writer, I was moved to a desk near the door to his conference room. As soon as I had set up my new desk, Mark asked me to step into his office.

"I want you to write an email to the company in my voice announcing that you've moved into this position," he explained.

"Okay," I said. "Is there anything in particular that you want me to mention?" I asked.

"I think just tell the positions you've had and what you're going to be working on," he replied. "It's a good story," he added with a grin.

"Yes, it is," I thought, and smiled back. This was the inexorability of Facebook, the desire it seemed to have ever since the launch of News Feed, the desire to turn everything into a story.

Now, as I suppose we all always were on Facebook, I was the story.

Sam stopped by my new desk as I was writing the announcement to ask what I was doing there, and I told him I was going to be writing for Mark. Even Sam, who usually approached everything with deadpan irony, seemed surprised at this almost pitch-perfect, sitcom-like outcome, in which the odd literary one becomes the new power player. He recovered quickly and we laughed together as always, then he jumped on a ripstik and skated off, leaving me to my email-writing.

"Hey Everyone—" I began. "I wanted to congratulate everyone on the fact that we reached 150 million users last week. This is an important milestone and reaching it shows how well we are doing at executing on our mission of making the world more open and connected. We're really just at the beginning, though, and we have so much more to do. I also want to make a couple of announcements. One is that Kate Losse, who began in Customer Support in 2005 and has since contributed to the Platform and Internationalization teams, is going to be taking on a role as Writer . . ." This isn't hard, I thought. You just need to sound like everything is easy, like everything happens as it should. At Facebook, I remember thinking at various points along this journey, the world is simple.

When I wasn't writing for Mark, I was watching the comings and goings of executives and visitors, wondering what decisions were being made that I would have to quickly catch up on and write about. I paid particular attention whenever unfamiliar and important-looking new businessmen came to the office, as that usually meant that some deal was going down that would have to be announced to the company later, such as when a group of Russians rolled in with the vague, almost fake-sounding name Digital Sky Technologies and invested in Facebook in May 2009. Mark's days were made up of constant meetings, whether with businessmen in blazers or Facebook product engineers, streams of young men in jeans and tight T-shirts marching nervously in and out of his office on the hour, laptops in hand. I was invited to attend his weekly executive team meetings, but only to, as Elliot told me, absorb Mark's thoughts.

In the first executive meeting I attended that January, Mark, Elliot, and Sheryl discussed the Twitter threat. Mark, who was usually sanguine, was quite nervous about the speed with which Twitter was picking up users and press, beginning in 2009 with about 7 million user accounts and rapidly *hockey sticking,* as rapid growth is called in the valley (up to about 70 million users by the end of 2009). Twitter threatened to be a faster, simpler, more efficient way of posting information to a wide public. As it turned out, the hunger for social media was big enough to accommodate both Facebook and Twitter, along with a host of later apps like Instagram and Foursquare that provide slightly different variations on ways to post and distribute to an audience.

I listened to Mark and Sheryl discuss the threat and what could be done to stop it, and whether it was something to worry about. At points I wanted to chime in, and began to do so, but saw Mark and Sheryl's displeased looks and quickly realized that I wasn't really supposed to speak. This was a power and a status game, after all, and even the highest executives were playing. Everyone in their place. So, I just listened, staring out at the rooftops of Palo Alto and playing with a loose piece of rubber on my Vans. We will be fine, I thought, Twitter doesn't have any native pictures; it's just text. Facebook, as the boys taught me, was all about the faces: the pictures, the video nation, mapping a world.

Eventually, after a month or so, once I had supposedly absorbed enough of Mark's ideas and mannerisms, I wasn't invited to the executive meetings anymore, but I didn't mind. I had begun to realize that aside from the blog posts that I was occasionally called on at midnight or seven in the morning to write, I didn't have much to write. Around then, many early Facebook employees' jobs, like mine, had become mainly to serve as the trusted, familiar faces of the company, and sometimes, in the boys' case, to serve as a research and development arm for our culture, which the company was so intent on preserving.

For example, on a designer's birthday, his friends rented sumo fat suits and held wrestling matches in the yard, posting hundreds of pictures on Facebook, which showed up in all of our News Feeds due to the heavy activity of people liking them. This is what in Silicon Valley is called a *proof of concept,* proving via the metrics, which in this case are high numbers of likes, that sumo suits at parties are a cultural hit. So, at the next Facebook company party, the party planners rented the same suits and made sumo wrestling into a company party game.

By the same logic, when Thrax wore an American Apparel track jacket to work, Facebook bought one for everyone in the company to wear. For years, some people wore them every day, walking around in matching jersey track jackets like an enormous high-school sports program. In this way, Facebook (and increasingly, the valley's) fascination with what was cool could make for a certain kind of career strategy: If you had the right look and played the right games, you could play all the way to the bank.

In the late spring of 2009, we moved to a new, sprawling campus in an old Hewlett-Packard building. Mark's desk was purposefully positioned in the building's dead center, on the lower floor, nearly underground. He called the building a bunker. We were starting to dominate the social media game completely now, to Mark's sometime chagrin. While he wanted to win, he preferred us always to be in a state of emergency, on lockdown, so that we had to devote ourselves entirely to the company and its mission.

Sometimes, when people didn't feel stressed enough, he called official lockdown periods, during which employees were required to work on weekends and late into the night. Lockdown periods were often called when some new, other social product, like Foursquare or Tumblr, came on the scene and we needed to mount some serious resistance by incorporating a version of it into Facebook's feature set, like the Places product (Facebook's answer to Foursquare, which was eventually superseded by general location tagging similar to that of Google+ or Twitter). Whereas, in 2006, the social network field consisted only of MySpace and Facebook (and a dwindling Friendster), by 2009 and onward, the social application field was becoming increasingly crowded, as many more entrepreneurs and programmers and investors got into the game.

The catch for Facebook was that the more successful we became (and we were still, despite all the competition, dominant), the more likely employees were to be distracted by money and the new pastimes it enabled: fine dining, bar hopping, five-star vacations, expensive cars. In this sense, winning the game completely was a bit of a curse, because as our user numbers climbed quickly to 250 million in July 2009 and 350 million in December 2009, early employees had less incentive to work constantly, and more leeway to play games and party earlier in the night instead of waiting until the dead hours of two in the morning to socialize like we used to. New engineers were being hired all the time to take up the slack of bug fixing and code development from employees who had been there longer. The Facebook product itself made staying on task difficult: With the steady stream of pictures flowing down our pages, how could we be expected to focus on anything but planning our next photo opportunities and status updates? Looking cool, rich, and well-liked was actually our job, and that job took a lot of work.

Late that summer, employees were invited to sell up to a quarter of our stock to Digital Sky Technologies, the Russian group who had invested in the company. The Internet whispered that some of their money came from a Russian mobster with a violent past. However, when the stock sale was announced at our weekly All Hands, no one asked if the Russians' money was clean and any questions that even skirted around the topic of who they were and where they came from got what is called a *hand-wavy* answer in Silicon Valley: a brushed off nonanswer at best. Transparency may be Facebook's business, but there were some things that no one wanted or was allowed to know. One way or another, the Russians cleaned up on their investment:

Five months after we sold our stock to them the stock had tripled in price, and one of the investors had purchased a $30 million mansion in Silicon Valley.

With the new rush of money came not just new activities but increasing power and attention. Celebrities like Katy Perry and Tyra Banks stopped by regularly to take tours of the office with Mark, and employees would stop what they were doing to take pictures and post them to Facebook. All of Facebook's Hollywood dreams were coming true.

Like any power mogul, Mark's desk in the bunker was surrounded by the work stations of people he liked and had fashioned as his closest deputies. At his pod were Schrep, the engineering director, and Chris Cox, the product director, both affable white guys with friendly faces. Sheryl kept a neat desk next to mine, a few feet away from Mark's pod. Her desk, as cool and efficient as she was, held a conference phone and digital pictures of her children and husband. She spent her time either in meetings with high-powered executives or on the phone with them at her desk, which I couldn't help but overhear. I admired her firm yet dulcet phone voice, which could be both decisive and quiet at the same time. She enunciated precisely, so as to make every thought seem like a decision, like the matter was always closed and the conversation had always already reached its resolution. It was comforting to imagine the world as it sounded in Sheryl's voice: a world where every question is already answered, where efficiency is assumed, where we all, like her, are on the path toward or have already made it to the executive suite.

The floor around Sheryl's desk was piled with the endless gifts that she received from business contacts in lofty positions at Fortune 500 companies. People sent her Louboutin heels and Frette candles the diameter of dinner plates, which she unpacked while on speakerphone with some CEO or another. Sometimes, she passed them over the desk to me offhandedly, just trying to get rid of them, but usually they just sat in piles under the desk until someone cleared them away, to be replaced by new, just as superfluous, luxury gifts. Mark's desk was similarly surrounded by boxes and gifts, but they were more boyish: a sports jersey signed by a soccer star, some video game that hadn't been released yet. I didn't have any presents (other than Sheryl's castoffs), but I had a front-row view of the business lives of the extremely rich and powerful, whom I now knew spend much of their days managing the world's desire to be close to them.

Once again, six months after the move to the new office, Thrax and I were thrown together. I was informed by Chase, who came by to tell me, with the same smirk he always had when trying to get us to hook up, that Thrax was moving in to my pod. "Oh," I replied coolly, but thought to myself, "Lol, of course." Sometimes, Facebook was like the world's most well-funded preschool, as if we were all sitting around playing with our Matchbox cars and singing "So and so and so and so sitting in a tree, k-i-s-s-i-n-g." We even had ants on a log at snack time sometimes, which was funny enough to me to capture in a photo and post on Facebook. Thrax's new job was to be Mark's technical advisor, where I was Mark's writing advisor.

These were recent roles that Mark had invented, jobs that

were not so much about doing things as being something, some version of Facebook that he wanted us all to personify. It felt as if the company's drive to convert us all into characters for the world's consumption was part of what was leading to the creation of these new roles. While Mark delighted in Facebook's ability to create infinite stories and characters, he didn't want to be the only character associated with the network. He wanted company in his position as the leader of our new social media enterprise. I felt sympathetic and almost protective of him in this impulse, as I privately always had: It must be hard to be a figure that everyone expects to represent an entire paradigm shift, a new and virtual way of being. Mark, with his preternatural, abstract focus on data and systems, needed charismatic, likeable people to share in this burden. Also, perhaps, I wondered if Thrax and I had by some accident of personality personified Mark's idea of what Facebook culture was: sarcastic sponges soaking up and performing all the American culture we could find. And, most important for Mark, we shared an impish delight in conquering.

Thrax arrived in the late afternoon, as usual, and piled his new desk with games, digital components that I couldn't identify, and books. The books were a comically academic touch for someone meant to serve as the face of education's new irrelevance to success. "Hey," he said, grinning, and I returned, "Hey," as the administrative assistants watched. I felt a sudden urge to turn to my screen and resort to IM to communicate, rather than sitting here and chatting as though we were colleagues working at real desk jobs, which I wasn't sure was accurate, sandwiched as I was between Sheryl's piles of luxury gifts and Thrax's electronic toys.

Mark's office sat adjacent to our pod, with its secret back room (for especially important meetings, because the front room of his office had a glass window onto the hallway that made meetings transparent) hidden behind a wallpapered door and a single table illuminated by a *Mad Men*–style modern lamp, receiving a constant stream of celebrities and tech luminaries and wealthy Russians in silk suits.

As at the summer house years before, Thrax's and my schedules rarely overlapped, as I left the office in the late afternoon just as he was waking up and arriving at work. When he was there, he received a steady stream of engineers coming to pay their respects, to trade jokes, and to ask him to play video games or go out that weekend. The constant visitors trekking through the center of the office—executives, celebrities, endless young men in hoodies—were another reason that accomplishing any actual work was nearly impossible. We mostly just sent instant messages and read Facebook and trafficked in lulz. When Kai came by one day looking for Mark and Sheryl and they weren't there, I said in character, "They're gone, I got rid of them," like a demonic child, and he said, "Good," and we laughed. Always be trolling.

Behind our pod were circles of desks, beginning with Mark's preferred engineers, like William, a skinny Stanford grad with longish curls whom all the boys claimed to have man crushes on, due to his immaculate code. Behind him was a set of newly graduated, mostly white engineers from Stanford and Harvard who were emerging to take the places of the now departed engineers who formed the first fraternity class at Facebook. Behind them in rows were many Asian and South Asian faces working on infrastructure, mostly people I had never met, many of whom spoke to each other in languages other than English. Some of them worked so far back in the building that their desks sat in windowless rooms, invisible and far from the endless games of ripstiking and chess that went on in the center of the floor. I was thankful for their work because, without them, nothing would ever get built or fixed. The Ivy League engineers, who formed the All-American window dressing of the company, were too busy making Facebook feel like what it originally was: a youthful, half-hacker and half–Ivy League enterprise, populated with smooth white faces, native and familiar.

One aspect of my job was to post updates to Mark's Facebook fan page, which, like writing his blog posts, was a fun puzzle, an impersonation challenge. I took pictures in the office and from the travel albums on his personal Facebook page and constructed spare captions in his voice, sticking to his main themes of information flow and changing the world. Cool-sounding posts about world travel and company news were easy to write: No one can argue with a photograph of a beautiful mountain or an historic site. But, when it came to posting to my own profile, the answer to the question of what to say and how to say it was increasingly unclear. I wanted to be authentic. I wanted to say something real. Facebook tells us to share "What's on your mind?" so it should have been easy, shouldn't it, to just say what I feel? But the prompt, and the system of liking and ranking that it feeds, always gave me pause. I was not sure whether the idea of sharing was that easy.

Facebook employees tended to post about their good fortunes and their increasingly glamorous lives at the company.

They also acted as Facebook's constant cheerleaders, posting news articles about the company, photos of employees at work, and celebrating the latest user growth numbers and feature launches. They believed, or seemed to, that the smallest, luckiest details of our lives were of utmost importance to share with the world, despite the fact that, since the stock crash in 2008, the global economy was slipping further into insolvency. To read their posts about fine dining, new cars, and luxury vacations, few employees seemed very concerned or aware of the deepening financial crisis. There was only one exception to this rule of sharing: No one ever posted anything critical of the company on Facebook. It would be like committing treason, to question the thing that fed us, both with food and attention and with a continuous drip of information. Facebook wanted us, like all of its users, to depend on it.

As 2009 progressed, I learned, both offhand and in closed rooms, that there were those who shared my skepticism about our goal of transforming the world into a virtual theater of ourselves. All that spring and summer, a team of product engineers worked on a remodel of Facebook's privacy settings that, unlike previous models, made certain information, like one's profile photo and friend list, public. This meant that absolute privacy from strangers on Facebook, which was the thing that I first originally loved about the site, as compared to sites like MySpace, would finally be obsolete.

Mark's reasoning for this move was in line with his general vision of the world and where it was going, as he often put it. "We are pushing the world in the direction of making it a more open and transparent place," he would say at All Hands meetings, "this is where the world is going and at Facebook we need to lead in that direction." A guy on the PR team that I worked with sometimes mentioned this change as we stood around drinking beer at happy hour. "I don't think that I want Facebook or any site to push me to be 'more open.' What does that even mean?" he wondered. I agreed that it was an opaque and strange concept. Forcing people to be more open implied that we were all in some way closed, as though there was something wrong in the way we conducted our personal lives. How was it a Web site's place to say that we needed to reveal more about ourselves publicly? Why couldn't Facebook just let people share as much as they were comfortable with?

Most employees I talked with seemed not to be particularly bothered by the company's decision to forcibly adjust people's expectations of privacy, preferring instead to focus on the light and almost childlike-sounding goals of sharing and connecting people. "She just doesn't get it," a user support manager told me about one employee who was soon to be terminated. "She doesn't believe in the mission. She thinks that Facebook is for people without any real problems and isn't actually changing the world. Can you believe that? This afternoon I'm going to have to let her go."

I wondered who the heretic employee was. I guessed that she must have been like all of the user support team members: well-educated in the humanities at an Ivy League school, and probably unaware when hired that she had walked into a new kind of technical cult. At any rate, her awareness of issues beyond Facebook was a problem. The company wasn't paying anyone to be aware of the world beyond the screen. The only questions you were supposed to ask or ideas you were supposed to have at work, as a good citizen of the Facebook nation, were about new ways to technologize daily life, new ways to route our lives through the web.

One afternoon in his office, Mark asked me to detail his thoughts on what he deemed to be "the way the world was going." "I have a series of blog posts in mind that I'd like you to write, I'd like to you to write a post on each idea, so people can understand what we are trying to do at Facebook," he explained.

"Okay," I said. "Shoot," taking out my Facebook-branded notepad to jot everything down.

"These are the topics I'd like you to write about," Mark said, listing them off. "Revolutions and giving people the power to share; openness as a force in our generation; moving from countries to companies; everyone becoming developers and how we support that; net-native generation of companies; young people building companies; purpose-driven companies; starting Facebook as a small project and big theory."

"Uh, okay," I said, feeling a bit overwhelmed. I was not quite sure what all of this meant to Mark or what I was supposed to do with it. I thought it was interesting that he was still into "revolutions," as was I, but his list then veered into territory I wasn't sure about.

"What does 'companies over countries' mean?" I asked, starting with the first one that jumped out at me.

"It means that the best thing to do now, if you want to change the world, is to start a company. It's the best model for getting things done and bringing your vision to the world." He said this with what sounded like an interesting dismissal of the other models of changing the world. I could imagine, like he may have, that countries were archaic, small, confined to one area or charter. On the other hand, companies—in the age of globalization—can be everywhere, total, unregulated by any particular government constitution or an electorate. Companies can go where no single country has gone before. "I think we are moving to a world in which we all become cells in a single organism, where we can communicate automatically and can all work together seamlessly," he said, by way of explaining the end goal of Facebook's "big theory."

"Okay, I'll think about these and get to work," I said. A set of designers were waiting with laptops in hand outside the glass-walled room, so we wound up the meeting and I went back to my desk.

I liked the idea of constructing philosophical blog posts, but when faced with Mark's topics I felt a curious sense of displacement, like I couldn't do this even if I tried. "I may not be really sure what Mark means by this, but I know I don't believe in it," I thought to myself as I walked back to my desk. It sounded like he was arguing for a kind of nouveau totalitarianism, in which the world would become a technical, privately owned network run by young "technical" people who believe wholeheartedly in technology's and their own inherent goodness, and in which every technical advancement is heralded as a step forward for humanity. But that reasoning was deeply flawed. While technology can be useful, it is not God; it is not always neutral or beneficent. Technology carries with it all the biases of the people who make it, so simply making the world more technical was not going to save us. We still have to think for ourselves, experience the world in reality as well as online, and care about one another as people as well as nodes in a graph, if we are going to remain human. And finally, I wasn't sure I wanted to be one of many "cells in a single organism." I liked my autonomy, my privacy, the fact that I was different from everyone else—a unique individual.

These thoughts brought me as close to philosophical debate as I had been since graduate school, which was fun. But when it came to the prospect of writing for Mark on these topics, it felt close to impossible. These philosophies, while interesting and provocative, weren't the ones I could write. They presumed some kind of beneficence of technology and its makers that, having spent years at the heart of the Facebook machine, I knew not to put my entire faith in. It's not that the people making technology were bad. They were just no better than anyone else when it came to understanding humanity and what we need, and giving them the power to decide what we—you, me, people we've never met—need as humans didn't seem like the wisest choice. But then, wisdom is not what technology is about. Technology is about solving things another way; without experiencing the problems, without afterthought, without having to do much at all. Technology can do these things for you so you don't have to. Sometimes, that can be helpful. Other times, I think that by using technology to accomplish our human goals we end up missing out.

After days and weeks spent mulling over these topics and their implications, I finally came to the conclusion that if Mark believed those things are true, he was going to have to convince people of them himself. The issue wasn't one of eloquence— simply writing well, which was my task as Mark's writer. The question was what did any of these values actually mean, and why should we want them? This was something only Mark could explain. I told him that I was having trouble coming up with satisfactory essays on the topics he'd assigned, and asked him to schedule time to explain his ideas in more detail, but he was too busy or wasn't inclined to explain further—it was hard to tell. I came to the conclusion that perhaps he thought I could invent these arguments of whole cloth, or that we already were cells in a single organism and I should be attuned enough to intuit what he meant, but I couldn't, and so the essays were never written or posted.

Although I liked my new job, I was unsettled as ever by Facebook and the valley's imperative to technologize everything. Having lived in this world of endless photographs and rankings and updates for years, I had begun to notice that, whether or not there was a correlation, my real-world relationships were becoming anorexic, starved of presence. I didn't know anyone in the Bay Area—Facebook employee or not—who didn't obsessively read their social media feeds and construct real and online conversations almost entirely out of these threads. "Did you see that post on Facebook?" or "I saw your tweet," they'd say. In this way, our posts and public presence online had become the inexorable, primary topic of discussion, rather than anything private or intimate or in person. If you weren't playing in the public sphere, sporting about on the social media field while everyone watched and clapped, it was as though you didn't exist.

I knew that if tomorrow I stopped updating my social networks with the ephemera of my tastes and thoughts, no one in the Bay Area would think of me. Even in the office, where I would spend six or more hours a day, I felt more visible online than off. People were too busy reading their screens to talk to each other.

That spring, a new Facebook engineer, not yet indoctrinated into Facebook's culture of the virtual, suggested a new feature. "I have an idea," he posted on the internal discussion board, "it would be a feature that allows you to suggest to two friends who don't know each other that they should meet and hang out." A veteran Facebook engineer jumped on the thread quickly to correct him. "We already have that feature," he said, "it's called the Friend Suggestion feature, where you can suggest that two people become friends on Facebook." "No, I meant a feature where you could tell two friends to hang out in real life. . . . Oh, never mind," the new engineer said, giving up.

Incidents like these, and the contentment people at work seemed to feel as they gazed, mesmerized, at their thirty-inch monitors, made me realize finally that this—Facebook, social media, our apps and phones and screens—was never really about real social life or interaction. Social media is about bringing us online and asking us to play with one another in digital space. Social media then is the ultimate Internet game, played according to the rules and metrics created by the boys who make the games and write their algorithms.

However, it was also as if the boys who knew the Internet best also knew that there was something dark about it, about this drive to have everything while revealing nothing. This, I think, is why they trolled, for trolling in itself is a kind of admission that we can't win online as our true selves, that authenticity online makes us too vulnerable, that vulnerability (or "vulns," as the hackers say) can be exploited too easily in an online world in which information is so widely connected and distributed.

Trolling, I decided, was the native mode of the Internet, and not exactly sharing in the literal way that Facebook declares it. Sharing is complicated and private; humor is entertaining, appropriate to an audience. Neither Mark nor any of the boys said anything that particularly revealed their emotions, for the most part. In fact, it was from them that I figured out early on that serious posts were kind of beside the point, despite Facebook's business need for us to post transparently about our lives.

So, I would troll instead. However, as a girl, I knew I couldn't troll exactly like the tech boys. I didn't want to post indignantly about how some new device or code upgrade was doing it wrong. I decided that, if I were going to troll, I would have to go at it from the opposite direction. Rather than trolling with technical details, I began trolling with a fatuous, un-articulated emotion that the boys could never get away with. "<3333333333333333333333," I posted as my status regularly, sometimes <3-ing particular things and people, with an exuberance that seemed infectious, for my coworkers began doing the same thing. Though I had begun posting hearts on everything as a joke, soon everyone in the office was earnestly decorating their Facebook posts with little hearts, skipping language, hardly bothering to comment anymore. It was if at some level we all intuited that "<3," whether intended earnestly or as lulz, was all anyone was looking for anyway and so, Facebook, with its ubiquitous like buttons and comments became a race to bestow and harvest as much digital love as possible.

Around this time, Facebook was testing a feature whereby users could reward each other with Facebook credits (Facebook's virtual currency, in which one credit equaled one dollar) for posting something particularly entertaining. Rather than rewarding one another by posting <3s in our comments, we could now reward each other with actual money. For the engineers who created the feature, it was as if the two were the same, and the guys in the office participated in the test happily, posting credits along with their comments. Thrax, ever shrewd, decided to take advantage. "This is a stickup, give me all your credits," he posted as his status one day. The guys in the office, realizing with delight that they had been expertly trolled, handed over their credits to Thrax in the comments under the post. As I watched the stickup transpire in my News Feed, I felt a certain awe. We had finally, literally created an economy of love, in which friendship and affection had a monetary value and a system for transacting it. However, engineers seemed more excited about trading credits to one another as a form of affection than anyone else at the company did, and the adding credits to comments feature was never launched.

"Miss u," master troll Carles of the blog Hipster Runoff said often, to and about everything, in his daily musings on Internet and popular culture that I read daily at work. Missing, I started to think, was the one true emotion of the Internet. In communicating primarily virtually we are always missing things, missing each other's points and missing out on the experiences of being with each other. So, I began to post that I missed things—

people, places, brands, states of mind—as much or more as I <3ed them. The only thing we never missed was our screens, staring back at us always, ready to make us feel just slightly less alone. "Miss u, real life," I could have posted, but few people at work would have gotten it. Real life was something everyone in my News Feed seemed relieved to leave behind, if only for the immediate reason that real life can't be owned and graphed and, as such, can't make you famous and rich.

If success is measured, as it is on the Internet, by memes spread and likes garnered, my Facebook trolling persona was successful, but my real life in Palo Alto remained an uneventful routine of work punctuated by runs on the Stanford campus, which swarmed with students dreaming of their own Silicon Valley success story. So, in early 2009, I decided to move to San Francisco and commute daily to Palo Alto. I found a room in an apartment at a messy end of the Mission that had been migrating from a working class to a digital class neighborhood for ten years. I was so excited to start over in the city that I didn't mind the fact that in the old Victorian I'd be sharing with two roommates the fridge door barely opened and the sills were caked with dust so thick that it might predate the 1906 earthquake (which the house, auspiciously for us if there were to be another earthquake, survived).

However, it was 2009 and, unlike in bohemian times, the past was never really behind us, just as the present was a different place than it used to be. Technology didn't really want us to ever leave things behind: We were expected instead to carry the past with us, all the time, in the form of pictures and tags and the smiling avatars of every person we have ever met, whether or not we still cared for them and they for us. The information was just there, populating, feeding, following us around as we conducted our lives. In this way, friendship never waxed or waned, but was always present in digital space. This was the eternal now of the Internet, and this, not Palo Alto or San Francisco, was where we had all begun to live.

Some weeks after I moved and was settled into my new place, Thrax asked me on AIM, "Do you want to go out in the city tonight?" He wanted to hang out because I'd left Palo Alto, in address at least. Men never want you to leave if they think you are really leaving. In this way, men and bosses are the same. And further, at Facebook, watching out for the boys was in a way my job, whether I wanted to hang out with them that night or not. "They are your boys," Mark's administrative assistant would say to me sometimes, implying that I shouldn't leave them entirely to their own devices, even though they were always up to their own devices, trolling and playing and judging, wielding their digital might. Devices, after all, was what it was all about, as Justin knew in advance when he spent all of Coachella struggling to receive a signal on his new, now completely outdated, BlackBerry Pearl.

"I'm tired, I woke up early today," I typed back to Thrax. I was tired because that morning I had to be at work at a somewhat normal working hour—ten o'clock—to star in a video detailing Facebook's completed internationalization process, which a documentary filmmaker had been hired to produce. "You are going to be the star of the film," the filmmaker had told me, and it reminded me of an old Hollywood scene of a starlet fresh off the bus from Iowa. "Are you a producer who is going to make me a star?" I felt like asking.

The shoot that morning had been long, the lights bright, and in my interviews I kept saying the wrong things—things that weren't peppy and fawning enough—and we kept having to reshoot scenes to get things right. I was not as good an actor on film as I was on Facebook, where I could craft my lines and persona in advance. So, by seven o'clock, I was tired and, like a Hollywood diva, I was already in bed.

"I'm wearing my pajamas already," I typed to Thrax.

"So am I," he typed back. "I just woke up. Let's go out."

Oh right, I remembered—the star engineers didn't have to go to work at all if they didn't want to. At this point, Thrax went to work maybe three days a week.

"Maybe," I typed. That's the thing now, with texting, you don't have to decide what you want to do until a second before. Technology enables an intoxicating degree of freedom, endless opportunities to do something or not.

An hour later, I had time to rest and get dressed, out of my pajamas and into a pair of jeans and a sweater. I flitted through the littered streets alone to meet Thrax; Ethan, a designer who lived near my new place in San Francisco; and a newer engineer, Liakos; at The Phone Booth, a dive bar on South Van Ness Street. It was a dirty, hip place, lit all in red and purposefully seedy, the scene of many Mission love crimes, I was sure. As always, the louche aura and grime of San Francisco were comfortingly authentic. In this bar, people could even smoke due to some archaic loophole in San Francisco smoking laws, adding to its stench of authenticity. I greeted the guys at the bar and ordered Fernet—an herbal, oily black liquor from Italy, popular in San Francisco for reasons no one knows—and went to put the Cure on the jukebox. It was a simple recipe for Mission happiness, as far as I was concerned.

I decided that I had good cause to celebrate with witchy drinks in darkest Mission: Improbably, I had come to occupy the highest position I could at the biggest tech company of the decade. I had become the boss himself, or at least his ventriloquist's voice. And while I could be scared—what if I fail, what if he fires me, what if they find out I don't wholly believe in our world-bending mission—I felt mostly just relieved. Everything that could have gone wrong already had, but I was still there and, unlikely as it might seem, I was winning. My stock options were starting to be worth enough that I could leave Facebook at any time and still have a livelihood. From then on, whatever happened at work wouldn't really matter.

The bar filled with taut-muscled gay men in leather jackets, like some movie version of New York in the 1970s. Inspired by their seventies vibes I played Fleetwood Mac songs on the jukebox and danced on the sticky dance floor. Amid all this vintage authenticity I forgot myself. "Second hand news," Lindsey sang on the jukebox, not referring to News Feed or any other form of mediated information, but to a different kind of connection that never seems to die. "When times go bad, when times go rough, let me lay you down in the tall grass and let me do my stuff."

After more Fernets and a lot of talk about Facebook and our aim to create what one of the boys excitedly called a new social operating system, Thrax and I walked back to my apartment on

Valencia Street. So did Liakos, who, like many of the Facebook engineers, followed Thrax's activity closely and seemed not to be able to bear to let him out of sight for a second. Thrax was as bewitching to his coworkers as to his distant Internet fans who followed his antics online. I could never tell, with all their liking and following of him and his online presence, if they wanted to be him or they wanted him. Was he their hero or their object of desire, and are those two things all that different when it comes to boys and their icons?

Silicon Valley's culture of the boy king made gay icons and followers out of people who aren't necessarily gay. Desire is strange, and our digital world made it even stranger, for we could consume and get off on anything we wanted, in any combination of people and things. As another Rule of the Internet reads: "There is porn of it," where "it" could be whatever fetish you desire, in any digital format: "There are no exceptions." The Internet has made it so that there are no limits to what we can do to gratify ourselves. If hackers are what you want, they are there for the watching.

But, that night, for once, we weren't on the Internet. I got blankets for Liakos and put him to bed on the living-room couch, leaving Thrax and me to sit cross-legged on my bed, talking. The Internet was missing, shut out of the action on my closed laptop that lay unused on the floor of my bedroom. "Welp. Miss u," I imagined the Internet saying to us from deep within some data center somewhere, perplexed as to why it had not been made master of ceremonies, router of all human affection and friendship. Thrax was there, and we were moving perilously close, almost to the point of kissing. Something had gotten into us to bring us to the brink of a physical consummation of our long affection. Perhaps it was the Fleetwood Mac, whispering to us from the free-and-easy seventies, fueled by real drugs instead of digital ones. "Players only love you when they're playing," Stevie sings in "Dreams," and I think that the song could be updated for the Internet age to read "Players only love you when you're playing."

"We should sleep in tomorrow," Thrax said. It was Tuesday, but neither of us had to be at work until we felt like it, which in his case could be as late as seven at night or never. Maybe it was the Fernet or the fact that in San Francisco we were far away from Facebook, but I felt bolder than usual, like I might finally be able to break the fourth wall, that barrier of virtual reality that we had built. Social media instead of television was our new fourth wall, and any true connection in the world we built required you to shatter the screen once and for all. "Okay," I said, snuggling out of my jeans.

Thrax leaned in to kiss me, and I almost laughed that this was actually happening, but it was. We were indeed breaking the fourth wall, as if the iPhone's tempered Corning glass was shattering everywhere, all over my bed, against Steve Jobs's and all the other tech titans' wishes that it stay unbreakable. Then, the siren of the virtual began to sing me back to its safe, contained shores. "I don't want to have sex," I declared.

"We don't have to have sex," he said, sounding mostly relieved. We were agreed, as always, that we didn't want to have sex. Sex with each other was too real. Horribly, chillingly real. Because from sex—the true, physical, total interlacing of bodies—you cannot go back to the virtual. The virtual was what our fortunes depended on. And, as figureheads of Facebook, we had to preserve the distance that the company depended on. For, if everyone were connected with the ones they loved, they—we—wouldn't need Facebook and its distant promise of love always somewhere around the corner. Real intimacy is the third rail of a publicity-driven, virtual society. We must avoid it at all costs. Thrax and I had always known this instinctively. Our unerring sense of control was what helped us win the game and take our seats next to Mark.

Something had to be done, though. Our odd, enduring affection was still there, always available to be picked up and left when it was convenient, like secondhand news. But I wanted—I needed—to try to kill it. I felt a sudden urge to destroy this—the tension, the war, the endless battle to be loved and liked—once and for all. If I could kill it, maybe I could check out and leave it all behind. And, so, I took charge.

The perpetual competition in our working and social lives reminded me of a line from a James Baldwin novel that seemed to illuminate all of this, this war for status, "Love is a battle, love is a war, love is a growing up," he wrote. Maybe for the boys, being loved was a war, a battle we wage on social media now, instead of in real life. And, maybe, whenever they tire of this game, love will have to be a growing up, something they'll have to find somewhere else, offline, away from the screen. So, in the unmonitored darkness of that night I decided it was okay, at least momentarily, to submit, and Thrax did too.

"Just don't update your status about this," I warned, eventually falling back onto my pillow.

"Hold on, I was just getting out my phone," he said, trolling.

"Not funny," I retorted, but we both laughed. It was funny.

Everything was. We were making a fortune out of broadcasting our own selves and interests to the world, and we didn't even have to go to work if we didn't want to. To punctuate this, my alarm clock began to chime errantly and we burst into more laughter. Who needs an alarm when you don't have to go to the office and when all this is over, you may never need to work again? The world was ours.

Or was it? When we did go back to work, the office and the computer screen and the crowds of virtual friends would be waiting to consume us, turning us again into totems of whatever it was they desired. For our distant audience, we always had to remain cool, in control. It was only for as long as the night held and we stayed asleep, spooned together like silver from the same set, that we could be unconscious of whatever the world was asking us to be for them. Perhaps in this world of digital surveillance and judgment, deep sleep was the only time when we were free. Maybe this was why, throughout the long climb to the top of Mark's virtual world, where winning everyone's adulation was our job, we always crawled into bed in the middle of the night, longing not for sex, but for some human presence that existed, silent and breathing, away from the screen.

CHAPTER 9

THE KING STAYS THE KING

*I*n July 2009, Mark was in Peru on vacation, contemplating whether I should join him on his press tour around Brazil. He knew nothing about Brazil and knew from my status updates that I did, so he listened to me when I told him how to wrest Brazil from Google's Orkut social network. Orkut had grown quickly in Brazil in 2006, unlike in other countries that approached online social networking more cautiously, because Brazilians took instantly and naturally to social networking of all kinds. I told Mark that, because Brazil's culture responds to personal contact, they might take Facebook more seriously if he paid them a visit in person.

"Mark is debating whether you should be flown out to Brazil for the press tour," his admin told me in the office that afternoon, only days before the tour began. I continued eating fork-fuls of lemon tart from my lunch plate. He would want me to be there, I thought to myself. This was just Mark's way of keeping me on edge and letting me know that he was in control. If it was an important decision he would have made it earlier, and quickly. "Okay," I said to her, "whatever he wants."

When I landed in São Paulo after the long flight, I was sur-prised to see a security detail made up of brawny ex-military men waiting to escort me to the hotel in a bulletproof van. The secu-rity detail loaded me and my luggage into the van and told me on the ride into the city about their earlier stints guarding Dick Cheney in Iraq. One had even served as Britney Spears's private security guard, and I asked him to tell me everything he knew about her. "She is really very nice," he said, "she always made sure the whole crew was fed, and would sometimes even buy us hamburgers." I was happy to hear that Britney Spears was nice.

The men in the detail turned serious only when we passed through a tunnel. "I hate tunnels," one growled tensely. "Why?" I asked. "Everything bad happens in tunnels," he said. "We learned that in Iraq. They can block you in on both sides and do anything they want to you in the middle," he explained. He only began to relax again when we emerged safely on the tun-nel's other side. "Everything bad happens in tunnels," I thought, reflecting on the past four years, Facebook's single-minded race to domination, and every strange, churlish thing that happened that I just had to shake off, because I was trapped in the middle and had to get through to the other side.

I like these security guys, I thought. It seemed healthy to be hanging out with people who had fought in real wars.

At the hotel, where an entire floor was reserved for Mark and his entourage, a member of the detail handed me a small pin to wear on my shirt. "This is in case there is an incident. We need to know who is one of ours so we can get you out of the place as soon as possible. No offense if we can't identify all the straps by face. The pin is more reliable."

"What are straps?" I asked, confused by all the security speak.

"You are the straps," they explained. "Mark is the package. He's number one, he's the guy we have to protect at all costs. Everyone else is the straps, because you're the hangers on. You're only important because he is, but we can't have you falling into the wrong hands." Lol, I thought. That was a good description of my entire job. I was only important because he is.

My room was all white, full of curved tropical modern furniture and a white marble bath with a round portal onto the São Paulo skyline. It felt, fittingly, like being in a room-sized white iPhone. I was glad that it all looked so modern, for Mark's sake. Whenever I mentioned my passion for Brazil to Americans they tended to think it is a lawless, third-world country where they will be kidnapped immediately. In reality, while violence does occur in some places, the country is rich and powerful, and Mark had to know this if Facebook was going to work at winning the country over.

We ate dinner that night at a high-end barbecue place, lush and very Brazilian, with open breezes and a beautiful tropical tree growing directly from the floor of the restaurant. I resumed a conversation that Mark and I had been having earlier about the fact that I thought it was unconscionable that we were not going to Rio on this trip. "I know São Paulo is the business capital," I said, "but Rio is the heart of Brazilian culture. Everyone knows this in Brazil, even the Paulistas who think that all people in Rio do is party and go to the beach all day. We cannot *not* go to Rio!" I was impassioned about this because my Portuguese professor at Johns Hopkins was a Carioca, or native of Rio de Janeiro, and the first thing she told us in class was that she was going to make us all Cariocas. My sudden vehemence about the Rio issue was proof that she had been successful. Even Mark seemed willing to be convinced. "Hmm, I'll think about it," he said, and actually seemed to be considering it. Well this is a first, I thought, that I could convince Mark to change his mind about anything.

I ordered us a round of caipiroskas, a national drink made of vodka mixed with fruit and sugar. Mark could barely drink his and called me crazy for drinking mine so easily. I shuddered to think what he would have thought of the nights in Brazil in 2005 when our Hopkins student group danced samba until morning, fueled by caipirinhas and the local beer. Some of us even did lines of coke in the bathroom. Mark would have passed out on sight. He hated drugs. I was told that he'd go pale at just the thought of them. At Facebook, we all knew never to even mention the word drugs near him. I made a mental note not to tell him that he was "the package," and that package means drugs in Baltimore slang.

However, there was no danger here of bumping into any drugs, samba clubs, or favelas: For the next few days, we were all business, visiting television studios and meeting with journalists on the rooftop restaurant at the hotel. One of these journalists, who, like a true, casual Carioca, wore a shirt printed with palm trees, said just as I had that we could *not* not go to Rio! Mark turned to me and said, "Whoa, you were right about this."

At one point, on a trip to the MTV Brasil studios across town, we had to stop in a park so that Mark could take an important, secret phone call. As he paced back and forth on the sidewalk, his security detail fanned out across the park, pretending to be strangers out for a walk. "They are like his 'muscle,'" I realized, as usual, entertaining myself by thinking of analogies to *The Wire*. Mark talked on the phone while his muscle tensely watched all the park's corners. The scene looked exactly like Stringer Bell taking calls in abandoned lots of Baltimore. Maybe, I thought, sitting in the van waiting for Mark to finish, he got to be Stringer after all: obsessed with business and winning, and perhaps not the one with the most heart, like Avon, but the one who got to the top.

The following day, we were sitting at lunch on the roof of the hotel with the skyline of São Paulo stretching as far as we could see when Mark declared imperially, as he gazed at the view, "We're going to write a book about Facebook together someday." That sounds fun, I thought, but then my mind reeled with questions. What would that book even be like? The book I would write about Facebook would be so different from the one Mark would write. It was weird that he assumed I thought the same way he did. My face must have betrayed my doubts and questions, because Mark looked at me with his typical coy smirk, and said, more directly than usual, "I don't know if I trust you."

You shouldn't, I thought, giving him a half-innocent look. But Mark's idea had planted a new one in my head. I could leave to write my own book, I thought. And after so many years of biting my tongue and speaking on behalf of Facebook, it would be a relief to finally speak and write as myself. After all, as *The Wire* teaches, you should never trust anyone, in business, at least. Keep your hackers close. Mark, who preferred to hire hackers, knew that. And at that moment, I felt almost, for a second, close to him, as if in the mutual ground of breaking into something— him, the business of registering the identities of everyone in the world, me, the company culture he had built—we had finally found a common bond.

And that was it. Like the security detail's van emerging from the tunnel, I felt like I wasn't locked in anymore. I could finally breathe. If Mark had figured out over lunch that I didn't believe and that I had a mind of my own, it didn't matter. Game over. And, who knows, perhaps he knew it all along.

Making the decision to leave Facebook, which, by the time I returned to Palo Alto in September, I was convinced I would do, and actually leaving Facebook, were two different things. Once one was that far into the company's tightly wound web of self-interest, in which everything we did was for the purposes of Facebook's god and country, you could not just put your security badge on your desk and walk out the door. First, there was the matter of appearances: How it would look. Facebook wanted everyone, especially its celebrated stars, to seem perpetually happy and gung-ho about the enterprise, and leaving implied that you weren't. Second, there was the matter of money: By the end of my career at Facebook, I was earning as much as a mid-to-senior-level engineer and, with that salary, had grown accustomed to luxuries that formerly were far out of reach. I had recently traded in my old Toyota Camry for a lightly used BMW 325i, which was the smallest and most entry-level BMW, but a BMW nonetheless. I liked eating Tartine pastries for breakfast and arugula salads and pasta at Beretta for dinner, none of which were cheap. I had become a card-carrying member of the San Francisco tech bourgeoisie, whether I loved technology or not, and, as I first noticed when I moved to the Bay Area in 2005 and was on the outside looking in, everything in that world— rent, smart-phone bills, restaurant meals, BMW payments, and Barneys purchases—was expensive. If I were to quit Facebook, I would need money.

Fortunately, my stock options had begun to develop significant value and, in 2009, a secondary market had sprung up in New York to trade in Facebook stock, despite the fact that the IPO was still far off. I found the number for SecondMarket on the Internet and retreated to a Facebook conference room to call them. I spoke quietly, wondering if the wires were tapped and assuming that they were, or that they at least could be listened in on if someone wanted to. At Facebook, you had to always assume surveillance, as that was our business.

The finance guys at SecondMarket were of course happy to hear from me and promised to arrange a sale. There was one caveat: In order to sell company stock prior to the IPO, one had to enter a byzantine process of paperwork, contracts, and lawyers, and one last stumbling block: Facebook had to be notified of the sale so that they could, if they chose, exercise what is called Right of First Refusal and purchase the stock back themselves.

By this point, I already knew for sure that I wanted to leave, so I said that it was fine, I would go ahead with a sale, even though Facebook would find out and I hadn't yet told them that I was leaving.

I knew that Facebook had been alerted that I was selling stock when I came to work several months later and Mark gave me a long, cold look. The friendly smirk was gone; I was no longer his bro. Sheryl gave me a similar look, not bothering to hide her disdain when we crossed paths in the bathroom later that day. I understood Mark's coldness: This company was his baby, and he had always been in control of it and, while we worked there, of us. It must be strange to see your dependents— people whose careers you have made possible, even as their long hours of work have helped your company prosper—asserting independence. However, the reactions of other executives and managers seemed strange to me. Don't they know this is just business—a huge, personal business, but business nonetheless? And, who was Sheryl, with her hundreds of millions of dollars, to begrudge a woman her first financial independence? I had worked for that stock, and now I needed it, because, unlike Mark and Sheryl, I was not already a multimillionaire. What for them was just extra, expendable wealth was, for me, money to live on. Whatever I was going to reap from my years at Facebook and my accumulated stock, Sheryl would reap more by a factor of millions. But, for them, I supposed, this really was by now all just a game, and they could afford to overlook any financial necessities, since they had bypassed the need for such considerations many millions of dollars ago. Sometimes, in the heady air of a bunker occupied by billionaires who could fund entire legacies solely on investment interest, it seemed like it was getting hard to breathe.

"I heard that you are selling stock," a manager on the PR team said to me in early 2010 after calling me into a tiny, airless conference room for a special meeting. "Yes," I replied slowly, thinking, "Are they going to stop me? Can they? Isn't the stock mine?"

"This really just makes me question your judgment," he said.

"You know, not everyone already has millions of dollars and can afford to wait years for Facebook to IPO," I explained.

"When people sell stock that means they are getting ready to leave," he countered.

Good, I thought, that means that I'm not the first person who has done this and it's a perfectly logical thing to do.

"I just don't know why you would want to leave," he continued. "Facebook has so much further to go; we're just getting started on our mission. This makes me think that you don't believe in our mission."

I began to feel like I was having flashbacks to television documentaries about church-cult indoctrination. Is he really talking about missions and not believing? I had heard this talk before (and had written some of it for Mark) but the fact that they were citing the mission and the question of believing just as I was trying to escape seemed extra creepy, as if this really were the Hotel California and even if I were running for the door, they weren't going to let me out.

To my chagrin, I burst into long-repressed tears, losing control after so many years of remaining stoic. "I can't believe that after everything I have done for this company you are treating me like this," I cried, my voice muffled by tears and mucus that were beginning to stream from my nose. "I know it's hard for you to believe, but not everyone is like you, not everyone wants to work for Facebook forever," I explained. "Some people want to leave and do something else. So, that's what I'm going to do."

"Okay, well, it seems you've made your decision," he concluded.

It was a bleary, undignified end to a long and, on balance, rewarding and exciting adventure, but at least it was finally the end. As a parting shot, Mark told his assistant to move my desk to another floor, removing me from his exalted engineering department, even though he knew my last day would only be weeks later. This was a symbolic gesture that relayed in no uncertain terms that I no longer belonged as a soldier in his technical empire, but, fortunately, I had already figured this out. I never even went to my new desk; I didn't know where Mark told his assistants to put it. In my last weeks, I came to work only to say my goodbyes, fill out exit paperwork, and eat the fine pastries prepared each day by the pastry chef. "Let them eat cake," I remembered thinking in 2006, when capital companies delivered cake to our offices, and indeed, as my last act as a member of the Facebook dynasty, that is what I did.

The day I left Facebook, in spring 2010, my life became instantly better, turning into a chillwave summer of nothing but late breakfasts at Tartine and long evenings at the park, the Phone Booth, or the Uptown, my favorite dive bars at which to talk and drink Fernet and listen to music on the jukebox. I hung out often with a new friend that I had met when he began following me on Tumblr. He listened as I talked about my recent departure from Facebook and the ideas I had about it that I wanted to write about. He had his own idea as to which television series closely corresponded to my experience. "You were like Peggy on *Mad Men*," he said, and I realized that, yes, it was kind of like that too.

In January 2011 I said goodbye to San Francisco and moved to Marfa, Texas, to write this book. Marfa, unlike San Francisco or Palo Alto, has no great need for the connectedness that we experience now over the Internet and on our phones, and perhaps that is why I was drawn here. In Marfa, it is the land and the sky, rather than any human enterprise, which scales, extending farther than the eye can comprehend, creating nightly sunsets that seem unworldly, even in contrast to any other sunsets one has been fortunate to watch. In Marfa, the ephemera of the social web recedes; it is the land and the art, like Donald Judd's one hundred sculptures in mill aluminum, that ask you to pay attention and consider them daily.

Marfa's disinterest in the social Internet isn't just metaphorical: The phones are slow for data retrieval, so posting a tweet or reading a feed is nearly impossible, at least from the phone. AT&T's lack of investment in data infrastructure there has similar effects to the town's lack of commercial and residential development, leaving the town in a masterfully preserved condition, as if the railroad age never left. Marfa, in fact, was founded as a function of the 1880s railroad boom: It was built to be a water stop for trains to take on water to make it across the next stretch of desert. I often found similarities between the railroad boom and Facebook: The builders of each made great fortunes by connecting with great centralized lines places that hadn't previously been connected, sometimes inventing things, like photo tags or Marfa, that weren't there before.

One night in January 2012, with nothing much else to do, my friends and I walked to an old Ice Plant left over from the railroad days, now turned into an art space, where a well-known artist from New York, Rob Fischer, had assembled a glass house on a trailer and suspended it from the ceiling. He proceeded to roll and swing the house by means of a pulley back and forth from one side of the ceiling to another, sometimes smashing it against the steel beams supporting the building. At one point, as I was videotaping this (old Facebook habits die hard), the house began to swing and roll and shimmy on the pulley ever more violently. At a brief lull in the house's movement, I turned off the camera, thinking I had captured all there was to be seen. Only a few seconds later, the house shifted violently, and one of its glass panes broke loose and slid the length of the house's floor only to crash out the other side, creating a beautiful (and dangerous) cascade of broken glass that fell just feet from where I was standing. Not one of the forty people in the room with cameras had captured that exact moment on video, though it was the unintended climax of the piece.

I think that this may be the truth of these technologies that we carry around: We film and post and read social media constantly in order to capture something, some exciting moment or feeling or experience that we are afraid to miss, but the things about life that we most want to capture may not be, in the end, capturable. And, perhaps, planning and efficiency themselves, the things that technologies like Facebook want to make easy and constant, are not as easily grasped as we think. Because, in all of our newfound efficiencies, what have we lost? What, like the moment at the Ice Plant when the glass shattered, is too unplanned and ephemeral to predict and capture with our technologies? Should we keep trying, or should we take a breath, and let some things go unshared and unrecorded, realizing that this ineffability may be the essence of life itself?

POSTSCRIPT

Thrax96: Are you living in Marfa?

K8che: Yes, are you in Austin?

Thrax96: Yeah.

Thrax96: Should we go in on a yacht?

Thrax96: Like a rapper video yacht

Thrax96: Except we actually own it, unlike rappers who rent it

K8che: Haha

Thrax96: Remember the multiple times we almost had sex?

K8che: Lol

Thrax96: Lol

Thrax96: In the land of the blind, the one eyed man is king.

K8che: Not sure what you mean. Is that a metaphor about you and technology? Like the camera on your iPhone and MacBook and how you were always filming? You were the king.

Thrax96: That was a double entendre.
Thrax96: One eyed man.
K8che: Oh, I get it.

I still think that's a metaphor about technology, I mused after I had signed off. "I'm going to put that in my book."

ACKNOWLEDGMENTS

*F*irst, I want to acknowledge my family for their love and encouragement.

I would like to thank everyone on my team at Free Press, including Dominick Anfuso, Daniella Wexler, Carisa Hays, Meg Cassidy, Nicole Judge, and Claire Kelley, for their enthusiasm and support for this book. In particular, I am very grateful to my editor, Alessandra Bastagli, for her great eye, judgment, and editorial vision; and to Melissa Flashman, for being a dauntless, loyal agent and friend.

I would also like to thank all of the friends, artists, writers, and places, many but not all of whom are mentioned in this book, from whom I have drawn inspiration and with whom I have felt connected in the course of my adventures. I am especially grateful to Dana Armstrong for her friendship, to Ashley Nebelsieck for her wit, to Owen for being my true bro, to

ACKNOWLEDGMENTS

Danish Aziz for listening, to Thrax for being there even when he wasn't there, to California for always shimmering off somewhere in the distance, to Baltimore for being my school of hard knocks, to Frank Ocean for being my 2011 muse when I needed one, and to Winter 2012 Marfa for all of its art and light.

Printed in the United States
By Bookmasters